D0902194

THE
DAILY
LECTIONARY

A weekly guide for
daily Bible reading
Advent through Eastertide
Year Two

With an introduction to the use of the Psalms
in the daily office

Joseph P. Russell

Contents

Printed in the United States of America for
Forward Movement Publicatons,
412 Sycamore Street, Cincinnati, Ohio 45202
and
C.C.S. Publishing Company,
628 South Main Street, Lima, Ohio 45804

Advent

This week we begin a new cycle of seasons, celebrations, festivals and selected lectionary readings. We turn from the last week of year 1 to begin reading with the first week of year 2.

Advent is a season that looks forward to the coming of Christ at the end of the age. At the same time, the season moves us back in our thinking to the time when our biblical ancestors were anticipating the coming of the new age of God, to be ushered in by the Messiah. It is a season that blends a heavy emphasis of penance with anticipatory joy at the coming of God. The joy, however, cannot be tasted without recognizing the bitterness of our sin. God will come to bring in a new day, but God will also come to judge our present day. What have we done with the life that God has given us? This is the penitential question of Advent that we must consider before we move to greet the new day.

As we concluded our course of readings during the late weeks after Pentecost, we noted the increasingly "apocalyptic" nature of the selections. Impending judgment and promise have been the themes expressed in our readings for several weeks. This increasingly apocalyptic message has also been characteristic of the Sunday lectionary readings for the Eucharist. The church has been preparing us for Advent. The seasons of the liturgical year follow the pattern set in the seasons of nature. We see signs of fall with the first turning of color, and then the fullness of fall arrives with colder winds that point, in turn, to winter. And so it is with our liturgical year. We see the colors of Advent forming with the late weeks after Pentecost that prepare us for the fullness of the Advent season that prepares us, in turn, for the wonder of Christmas.

The first week of Advent

The Old Testament readings:

Amos was a shepherd from the town of Tekoa in Judah. He lived in the eighth century before Christ. He felt a call from God to leave his life as a shepherd and go to the cities of the northern kingdom of Israel to call the people back to their covenant with God. Amos spoke words of harsh judgment condemning the people for drifting so far from the ways of the covenant. The Advent theme fits well with Amos, for in Advent we too are called back to the covenant. We too must stand in judgment before God and the prophets of God who confront us today. We must take Amos' words seriously if we are to live the Advent faith to which we are called.

In the opening section of Amos we find him condemning the surrounding nations for actions that displease the God of Israel. We can picture a crowd drawing closer to hear these words of judgment on neighboring peoples. We always like to hear the bad news about someone else. Each statement of judgment is followed by words of doom. God will act against a wayward people, Amos warns. But by verse 4, in chapter 2, Amos starts to move closer to home. He speaks out against Judah, a people once united with Israel. Finally in verse 6, Amos strikes home: "For three transgressions of Israel, and for four, I will not revoke the punishment. . ." Now the people standing at the town gate hear the judgment on themselves. They have no special status with God. They have no more standing, in fact, than the peoples around them who have transgressed God's intentions for all people.

Tuesday's text makes it clear that because God had chosen Israel to receive special favor, the people must bear an even greater judgment, for they rejected their unique relationship with God revealed to them in the wilderness. Then the text turns to a poem that builds on a theme of cause and effect: "Does a bird fall in a snare on the earth, when there is no trap for it?" A series of similar statements leads to the final statement: "The Lord God has spoken, who can but prophesy?" The surrounding nations are to assemble to see the evil that lies at the heart of God's people, Amos says rhetorically. He pronounces the ominous word that an adversary (Assyria) will soon surround the land and conquer it.

Beginning with chapter 4, read on Wednesday, the prophet outlines in poetic phrases the sins of Israel: "Hear this word, you cows of Bashan." This sarcastic reference was directed toward the wealthy women of the day who lounged on couches ordering their husbands to serve them more wine. Bashan was an area known for its large cows. Amos was undoubtedly a lonely man as he wandered the lands of Israel! He ridicules the empty worship practices of Israel in the closing words of Wednesday's text. Bethel and Gilgal were sacred places of worship. The people went there to transgress the law!

In Thursday's reading Amos points out all the danger signals of natural disaster that should have called the people back, but they did not listen to the signs. "Prepare to meet your God, O Israel," is a warning sometimes found scrawled on signs by the side of the road. The phrase originated with Amos as yet another warning to the people.

"Seek good, and not evil, that you may live," Amos urges the people (Amos 5:14). Saturday's reading contains some well known phrases. The people who have dreamed of the "day of the Lord" because they have seen it as a time of restoration will find it a day of doom instead, he warns. Then he calls them to true worship. God hates empty worship practices that don't lead to acts of justice: "Even though you offer me your burnt offerings and cereal offerings I will not accept them...But let justice roll down like waters, and righteousness like an ever-flowing stream." It is not the ritual of worship that Amos condemns, but rather worship without relationship to justice.

The Epistle readings:

This first week of Advent we move to one of the last of the epistles to be included in the New Testament. Second Peter could have been written as late as 140 AD. Someone who was influenced by the followers of the apostle Peter, rather than the apostle himself, was probably the author.

The message of the writer is crucially important to the new testament church. Christ has not returned. False teachers have come into the Christian communities with doctrines and interpretations of Christian writings that are leading people a-stray. Remember the promise of Christ, the writer urges. Don't lose hope in the Lord's return. You have a special calling as God's servant.

At the conclusion of Tuesday's reading, notice the warning about interpreting scripture. The individual cannot be trusted to understand scripture without the guidance of the Holy Spirit. This passage is one of the justifications the church used for many generations in attempting to control the reading and interpretation of scripture.

On Friday we leave 2 Peter and pick up the Epistle of Jude. This is appropriate since the two epistles were written at about the same time and deal with the same problems that had arisen in the second century church. "Stay with your teaching and faith as the solid foundation of your life," is the message of Jude.

We too grow tired, disillusioned, and are led astray into false teachings. Advent calls us back to the path and to the vision.

The Gospel readings:

Our readings in the gospel this week sound more like preparations for Easter than the first week of Advent. In previous prayer books, it was a tradition to read the triumphal entry account on the first Sunday of Advent for it symbolized the expectation that Christ will come again at the end of the age to both judge and redeem the people. And so we begin our Advent gospel reading with the entry of Jesus into Jerusalem. See it as pointing ahead in visionary time rather than backward in historic time. Let the past shape your vision of the future as you read of Jesus' words and actions. Remember that Advent points ahead to the coming of Christ. It is not merely a memory of birth, but a vision of coming birth for all peoples.

A little background is necessary to appreciate the cleansing of the Temple scene. Jesus was not upset with the money-changing and selling going on in the Temple. That was essential for the carrying on of the rites practiced there. It was the unfair practices that had grown up around the money-changing and sale of sacrificial animals that aroused his anger. But of more importance, Jesus was acting out a prophetic drama to announce the inauguration of the messianic age. Take a moment and read Jeremiah 7:1-16, Isaiah 56:7 and Malachi 3:3-5 so that you can see Jesus' activity in the same perspective as the people of his time. You may also want to read Jeremiah 13:1-11 and Isaiah 20:1-6 for examples of similar dramatic actions by the prophets.

The curse of the fig tree can best be understood as a parable told by Jesus (see Luke 13:6-9) that the writer of Matthew (and Mark) placed in the narrative to emphasize the point of what was happening in these final days.

Jesus' actions at the Temple were not lost on the authorities. They moved quickly to entrap him in order to discredit him among the people and to find grounds on which he could be brought before the Jewish and Roman courts.

The parable of the vineyard read on Thursday would have aroused the anger of the religious authorities instantly. Those who do not care for the vineyard will be cast out and others will be given rights as tenants. Read Isaiah 5:1-7 to see the inspiration for this parable. The parable of the wedding feast read on Friday confronts the institutional church of our own day. We, like the Jews of Jesus' time, are invited to be God's witnesses in the world, but it is often the outcasts whom God must bring in to sit at table. We are bound by our possessions and worldly responsibilities, too busy and involved to respond. Verses 11-14 seem to introduce a separate parable about a man who came to a wedding banquet without the proper dress. The point of this second parable differs from the first. Here the man is condemned because he had not prepared for the event. He, like the young maidens who did not purchase enough oil for the night watch, is thrown out into the night (see Matt 25:1-13).

Saturday's reference to paying taxes to Caesar is not meant to imply that there are two separated realms of responsibility in the world, the sacred and the secular. The "things that are God's" are everything in heaven and earth, if we take the Torah seriously. It is lawful to pay taxes to Caesar so long as Caesar does not contradict the ways of God.

5

The second week of Advent

The Old Testament readings:

The Torah demands compassion and justice for the poor of the land. It demands a concern for the welfare of the nation. But the wealthy, Amos points out in Sunday's reading, have forgotten their responsibility. They take their ease in fine homes living lavish, self-indulgent lives. If they just looked around them they could see the coming doom of the Assyrian invaders. Invasion by this foreign power will be God's judgment on a wayward people. It will be God who will raise up that enemy nation, Amos warns. The prophet foresees a time of such terrible desolation in the land that the people will be afraid to mention the name of God because they will be so terrified of God. Such is the punishment for breaking covenant.

From direct words of coming doom spoken to the people, our text shifts on Monday to a visionary dialogue between God and the prophet. Into Amos' mind come visions of coming destruction. He pleads with God to avert the sending of locusts and fire to destroy the people. Then Amos sees a vision in which God measures out Israel as a builder would measure the walls of a city. The plumb line would immediately show where something was "out of line," and so it is with God's people. They are "out of line" and God will ". . . never pass by them." That is, God will never forgive their transgressions. The destruction of Israel's sacred places by the invader's sword is the closing warning of Monday's reading.

Amos will not be silenced even when powerful men order him to cease speaking at the holy place of Bethel.

Locusts, fire, sword and now the innocent vision of a basket of summer fruit lead to Amos' next prediction of doom. The fruit is ripening. The day of God's wrath is drawing near. Amos levels one more charge of social injustice in the Wednesday lection. The rich trample upon the needy. They can't wait for the sun to set on the Sabbath so they can get back to their oppressive acts of economic injustice. Amos' writings are a reminder that acts of social and economic justice are the "plumb line" that we are measured by. Politics and religion do go together. The Bible always addresses the social questions of our times and not just questions of personal ethics.

The fifth and final vision of Amos is read on Thursday. The columns holding up the sanctuary are to be destroyed bringing the building crashing down upon the people. The scene of Samson shaking the columns and bringing down the Temple on the heads of the people comes to mind as we picture the destructive vision that comes to Amos (Judges 16:28-31). There is no place to hide from God and the destruction that is coming. If the people think they have a special relationship with God because of what God has done for them in the past, the prophet quickly dispels such hopes. Israel is like the other nations, he points out. God acts in the history of all people, and all nations are equally liable for their sins. The prophet saw beyond the limited nationalism of his time.

Many scholars feel that beginning with Amos 9:8, we have the writings of a later editor who added a postscript of hope to the severe words of Amos. Compare the feeling of Amos 9:8-15 with the rest of Amos' writings and draw your own conclusion. (Amos 9:11-15 is assigned for Sunday, providing words of hope.) Certainly there is a sudden change of tone beginning with the eighth verse: ". . . I will destroy it from the surface of the ground; except that I will not utterly destroy the house of Jacob." Instead, the coming destruction will be like sifting grain in a sieve. The righteous in Israel will not be destroyed, is the hopeful word.

On Friday and Saturday we read the short Book of Haggai. As Advent shades toward Christmas, our mood is lifted from warnings of judgment to words of vision for the coming of the Messiah. Haggai wrote during the time our Biblical ancestors were returning to Judah from Babylonian exile. The people had moved quickly to build their own homes upon their return, but the Temple still lay in ruins. Haggai's role was to urge the restoration of the Temple. The people are to have faith. They will be blessed by God again when they restore the Temple. Notice the references to a "remnant" people (1:14). The time in the exile was seen as a sifting. Only a remnant returned to their land. That remnant would form a new people faithful to God.

The second readings:

This week we begin a two-week reading of the first six chapters of the Revelation to John. Because so much confusion and mystery surround this book people tend to shy away from it, or they take it as literal prophecy of what is to come. Before we start to read Revelation we need to keep a few things in mind. Revelation is a distinctive type of literature called "apocalyptic" from the Greek word meaning to reveal or to uncover, as in uncovering a mystery. This unique style of literature, *The Interpereter's Bible Dictionary* tells us, originated in the Persian religious cults and gradually was taken into Jewish literary tradition during and after the Babylonian exile. Look over the Old Testament books of Daniel and Ezekiel and compare them with the material you will find in Revelation. (*Interpreter's Bible Dictionary,* Volume 1, Abingdon Press).

Apocalypticism rises out of an oppressed people who see their hopes dashed in the continuing oppression of foreign powers. These powers take on the characteristics of evil. The hope that gives courage to the people is that the power of God will finally defeat the power of evil and restore the faithful to a new kingdom prepared for them.

The coded nature of this style of literature hides the true meaning from the oppressor while giving hope to the oppressed. The Revelation of John was written about 95, during the reign of the Roman emperor, Domitian, an emperor who ruthlessly persecuted the Christian churches of the empire.

The great theme of Advent is picked up in the Monday's reading: "Behold, he is coming with the clouds. . ." (Rev 1:7). Christ comes to judge and Christ comes to save. The nations will tremble at the sight of the one who was pierced for the sins of the world. The people of Christ will rejoice over the day of total triumph.

On Tuesday we are introduced to the writer of Revelation, John of Patmos. The writer is unknown. Literary style and theological approach separate the writer from the writer of the Gospel of John or the epistles of John. We only know when this author wrote, for he gives us a historic picture of his time.

Symbolism is the medium he uses to convey his theological convictions. He provides us with sometimes beautiful, sometimes frightening and always awesome word pictures of the coming reign of Christ. We receive the first word picture on Tuesday. The triumphant Christ stands before the writer in an intense vision. Seven is the symbolic number used throughout the book. John's first order is to write to the seven churches represented by the seven lampstands. John becomes scribe for the exalted Christ writing to the seven angels who watch over the seven churches.

The churches of Ephesus, Smyrna, Pergamum, Thyatira, Sardis are addressed in this week's readings. Each one is given a critique of their faithfulness, and each one is found wanting in some way. Advent is a time when the "seven churches" of the world of today are called into an accounting before Christ. What would the judgment be for the church today? How would the scribe address us? That is precisely the theme of Advent expressed in vivid metaphor by the writer of Revelation.

The Gospel readings:

Jesus' controversey with the religious authorities of his day becomes more intense as we read from the Gospel of Matthew this week. Though the Pharisees believed in the resurrection, the Sadducees refused to accept the doctrine. Thus it is the Sadducees who seek to discredit Jesus on the subject of resurrection by raising an impossible problem arising out of the Law regarding a brother's responsibility to marry the wife of his deceased brother. Jesus' response moves the argument beyond life as we understand it today to life as God wills it for us in the age to come where marriage customs have no meaning. Jesus quotes from Exodus 4:15 to make the point that God spoke to Moses about the ancestors of the Jews as a living people: "Say this to the people of Israel, "The Lord, the God of your fathers, the God of Abraham, the God of Isaac, and the God of Jacob, has sent me to you. . ."

9

Tuesday's reading opens with words familiar from their use in The Book of Common Prayer: "You shall love the Lord your God with all your heart, and with all your soul, and with all your mind. This is the great and first commandment. And a second is like it, You shall love your neighbor as yourself. On these two commandments depend all the law and the prophets" (Matt 22:37-40). Note that these are not Jesus' own words; he quotes from Deuteronomy 6:4-5 and Leviticus 19:18.

The second part of Tuesday's reading (Matt 22:41-46) can be confusing as Jesus is again making subtle use of scripture to make his point. The Messiah expected by the Jews was to be a military hero who would drive out the enemy. He would be a descendant of King David. Psalm 110 was attributed to David as its author. In the verse quoted from the psalm David seems to be subservient to a greater "Lord." So how, Jesus, asks can the "Lord" or Messiah be David's son? "Enlarge your vision of the Messiah," Jesus is saying in this rather obscure passage. The Messiah is to be far more than a military hero, a son of King David.

From Wednesday through Friday we read strong words of denunciation against the religious authorities of Jesus' day. To feel the power of these words, we need to apply them to the religious authorities of our own day. How does the Church "...tithe mint and dill and cummin, and have neglected the weightier matters of the law, justice and mercy and faith..." (Matt 23:23)?

By the end of Advent we will be well versed on apocalyptic literature. The Book of Revelation is our second reading these two middle weeks of the season, and on Saturday we move into a section of the Gospel of Matthew that deals with Jesus' concerns about the end of the present age. The whole chapter is a collection of sayings and parables about the final times that will come before the new age is ushered in. If you want to impress your friends or Bible study companions, call this the "eschatological discourse." Eschatology is a technical term in theology meaning the last things of life, from the Greek work meaning last or extreme. These last times will be soon, Jesus warns. Struggle and persecution are seen by Jesus as a part of those final times. Though Jesus' words would have formed the basis of Matthew's writing, they also reflect the destruction of the Temple in Jerusalem that had just happened as Matthew wrote his gospel.

The third week of Advent

The Old Testament readings:

After Sunday's reading in Amos, we turn to the prophet Zechariah on Monday. He was a contemporary of Haggai with the same concern of rebuilding the Temple and in pointing toward the messianic age that he saw dawning with the rebuilding. Our reading in Revelation will help us appreciate the apocalyptic nature of Zechariah's writing. The language of vision and metaphor frames the theological expression of this book.

Our reading begins with the vision of four horsemen going out to patrol the earth. They report that all is quiet. God's punishment of the nations oppressing Judah has not yet begun. Judah has been punished with 70 years of exile in Babylonia, but soon she will be restored as God's favored nation. The rebuilding of the Temple will be a sign of that restoration.

Jerusalem can be a city without walls in the future restoration. She will live at peace and so many people will be drawn to the city that walls will not be able to contain them. Those who have oppressed Israel will in turn become the servants of Judah: "Sing and rejoice, O daughter of Zion; for lo, I come and I will dwell in the midst of you, says the Lord" (Zech 2:10). The promise of God again dwelling with the people has a Christmas ring to it.

In Wednesday's vision, God declares the Temple priesthood cleansed. That's the word Zechariah declares to the people in the colorful imagery of apocalypticism. Satan is not to be equated with the devil. In the visionary language of the day Satan was simply the figure of the prosecutor in the heavenly court bringing charges against the high priest who stood as defendant. In this scene, God declares the defendant innocent. His clothes, that denote sin, are replaced with new garments of joy and acceptance. Incidentally, John and Charles Wesley's mother quoted Zechariah 3:2 when she described their rescue from their burning home as an omen of God's favor toward them: "Is not this a brand plucked from the fire?"

We see where the writer of The Revelation to John got some of his symbols. Four horsemen, seven lampstands, seven eyes are all symbols Zechariah and other writers of the time used to express their message of vengeance and hope. Zerubbabel the king and Joshua the high priest are anointed by God to restore the people. For the cynics who said the rebuilding of the temple was an impossible hope, Zechariah responds that God's power will be shown through the Temple's completion. A mountain of impossible odds becomes a smooth plain with God's power evidenced in restoration.

Friday's reading is a reminder to the people of their just punishment in the past along with the promise of restoration in the future. The prophet paints a beautiful scene of perfect peace that is coming soon. The sight of old people is a sign that wars and pestilence will not be visited upon the people. Little children playing in the streets give hope for the future generations.

The reference to "remnant" comes up frequently in the writings of the post-exilic prophets. The remnant of the once great nation will be restored in ways never dreamed of in the past. Zechariah's message is summarized in Saturday's reading: "As I purposed to do evil to you, when your fathers provoked me to wrath, and I did not relent, says the Lord of hosts, so again have I purposed in these days to do good to Jerusalem and to the house of Judah; fear not" (Zech 8:14-15).

The second readings:

The letters to the seven churches continue this third week of Advent. Philadelphia stands before Christ and is found faithful: "I will keep you from the hour of trial which is coming on the whole world, to try those who dwell upon the earth." The contemporary version of the Lord's Prayer (BCP, p. 364) reflects these words well: "Save us from the time of trial, and deliver us from evil." The familiar words of the traditional form of the Lord's Prayer miss the impact of the petition: "And lead us not into temptation but deliver us from evil." The language has changed since the 16th century. When we pray the Lord's Prayer we need to keep in mind the Advent theme of Revelation and the words to the seven churches.

Laodicea is next before the judgment pen of the scribe. They are found wanting, lukewarm, neither hot nor cold: "Behold, I stand at the door and knock; if any one hears my voice and opens the door, I will come in to him and eat with him and he with me" (Rev 3:20). Sunday school pictures of Jesus knocking come to mind with this familiar phrase.

The scene shifts on Wednesday and we are lifted up to the throne of God. There we see a vivid scene of heavenly creatures worshiping God constantly. Read Isaiah 6:1-13 for the inspiration for this scene. The song of the heavenly chorus is the familiar, "Holy, holy, holy, is the Lord Almighty, who was and is, and is to come" (Rev 4:8). The "Sanctus" of the Holy Eucharist comes from these two sources. As we stand at the eucharistic table we join "...our voices with Angels and Archangels and with all the company of heaven who for ever sing this hymn to proclaim the glory of your name." In that moment we join in harmony with the heavenly chorus. We are part of the Isaiah and Revelation scene. We have momentarily stepped into the reign of God. Our worship community expands to include the heavens and earth joined in eternal praise.

Thursday we see the first of many canticles probably sung by the congregations of the writer's time. We find the first hymnbook of the church embedded in Revelation and other writings of the New Testament.

On Friday the imagery of Christ changes to the Lamb "...standing as though it had been slain." Only the Lamb is able to open the scroll that contains the plans of God. The power of the Lamb is shown in the symbols of horns and eyes that express the seven spirits of God sent to the earth. We see another early Christian hymn in the midst of Friday's reading. This hymn is canticle 18, appointed for Morning Prayer (BCP, p. 93). The Book of Revelation is a greater part of our worship experience than we may be aware of.

The trials of the end time referred to above begin with the breaking of the seals. Saturday's reading is grim. Four horsemen are released to bring pain and destruction to the earth. The first is a conquering invader, the second brings war and bloodshed, the third famine and the fourth brings disease and death. The martyrs are pictured "under the altar" crying for vengeance against their oppressors. Their cry is met with earthquakes and other natural disasters.

As you read these words remember that Revelation was written to give hope to Christians during a terrible persecution. As our Christian ancestors heard these words they began to see meaning in their struggle. God had a plan. The words of anger we read in Revelation match the anger often reflected by the psalmists of the Old Testament.

Revelation sets a mood for Advent, a mood that stands in contrast to the mood of our surrounding culture. The Advent season is to call the churches to account as the seven churches of Revelation were called to account. Advent is to help us make sense of our times. History unfolds in ways that seem so contrary to God's will, and yet God is victorious even in the midst of what appears to be destruction.

We will continue our reading from the Book of Revelation in mid-October.

The Gospel readings:

In 70 AD the Romans responded to a Jewish rebellion by destroying the Temple and the holy city. Jesus foresaw the destruction of Jerusalem that came after his death as a sign that the new age of God was dawning. Out of the ashes of the old the new kingdom of God would be built. The Temple in Jerusalem would be replaced by the living temple that is Jesus' presence in the world. (The indwelling of the Holy Spirit will make each person a living temple of God, St. Paul said in later years. See 1 Corinthians 6:19.) Jesus used the language of apocalypticism, familiar from our reading of Revelation, to describe the dawn of the new age. Read Daniel 12:1-3 for a flavor of this style of literature that lies behind Jesus' words as well as the colorful symbolism in Revelation. The thrust of the message is that God is soon going to intervene to bring the present age of darkness to an end and usher in a new age of God.

Three powerful parables of coming judgment fall in rapid succession Thursday, Friday and Saturday. All of them speak to the same concern. We must be ready for the coming of Christ. We will be judged on our readiness. We must be ready at every moment. Paul echoes Jesus' words when he wrote to the Christians in Rome: "Besides this you know what hour it is, how it is full time now for you to wake from sleep. For salvation is nearer to us now than when we first believed; the night is far gone, the day is at hand" (Rom 13:11-12).

The parable of the talents is not an encouragement for capitalism. We will not be judged by how much interest we've earned on our investments in this world. Rather it is a confrontation with how we perceive our gifts and the God who grants them to us. How much are we willing to risk for the sake of the gospel? It is interesting to note that the servant who hides his talent has a perception of the master that would keep *anyone* from risking. "Master, I knew you to be a hard man..." (Matt 25:24). The first two servants were not limited by such a perception.

The parable of the last judgment is a vivid statement about our call to live with constant concern for others. To feed the stranger is to respond to Christ.

The fourth week of Advent

The Old Testament readings:

This week before Christmas we read selections from several books that help us to frame the coming season of the Incarnation within the "get ready" context of Advent. The length of this fourth week of Advent, of course, will vary according to when Christmas falls.

Sunday we read the mythic account of woman's and man's separation from their intimate relationship with God. Adam and Eve stand before God estranged from themselves, from each other and most of all from God. Christ comes to heal the ancient wounds. Monday's reading is a glorious canticle of praise to God at the thought that God will dwell in the midst of the people. God will restore all peoples: ". . . I will save the lame and gather the outcast" (Zeph 3:19).

Tuesday's text is the song of Hannah. Compare the song of Mary, Luke 1:46-55, with Hannah's song. In both, the feeble and poor will be raised up. The proud and arrogant will be brought down. Jesus' birth in a stable and his life among the oppressed and suffering was a living out of the hymn.

Wednesday's reading is a promise to King David that ". . .your house and your kingdom shall be made sure for ever before me; your throne shall be established for ever" (2 Sam 7:16). David's prayer of joy and thankfulness for that promise is the content for Thursday's reading. These passages set the stage for understanding the role of Jesus whose birth and eternal presence among us we are about to celebrate.

Friday's reading comes from the apocryphal book of Baruch. Baruch, you may remember, was Jeremiah's secretary. This book purports to be the writing of that man who lived as Judah fell to the Babylonians, but it was probably written about 150 years before New Testament times. The writer gives us a psalm of hope for a coming restoration. The people will soon ". . .see your salvation by God" (Baruch 4:24). An appropriate reading for these moments before Christmas. The reading for December 24 is a continuation of this great song of hope. Supposedly written during the time of Babylonian Exile, Baruch pictures the people of Judah triumphantly returning to Jerusalem singing songs of joy. God will level the hills and raise up the valleys to make the journey easier. The writer drew on historic imagery to paint a picture of future salvation. He borrowed some of his images from the great prophets.

The portion of the Book of Isaiah read on Christmas Eve was written after the return of "the remnant" from Babylonian captivity. We come in on the end of a great dialogue between God and Judah. God has just condemned the people of their sinfulness. The people have responded with confession, and now God proclaims through the mouth of the prophet that nations alien to Judah have been destroyed because of the power of God's hand. God is armed with "righteousness as a breastplate...a helmet of salvation...garments of vengeance...and fury as a mantle." God's word will never depart from the mouths of Judah's coming generations. Restoration and salvation, words of God's presence and power, set the stage for our celebration of Christmas this evening.

The Epistle readings:

The first half of this week we spend in Titus. First and Second Timothy and Titus are called "pastoral epistles" because each deals with the pastoral concerns of the primitive church. Many scholars feel that though these epistles are attributed to Paul, in fact they were written by disciples of Paul at a later date.

Questions arise because Paul lived with the expectation that Christ would return soon; the pastoral epistles, on the other hand, seem to have been written at a time when Christians had modified this view.

Titus was a faithful disciple of Paul. We catch glimpses of their relationship in Galatians 2:1-3 and 2 Corinthians 8:6, 16-23. Though the letter opens with personal greetings to Titus from Paul, realize that the letter is really addressed to the whole emerging church, providing guidelines for structure, discipline and Christian witness.

Monday's reading includes criteria for choosing leaders that parallel the criteria found in the third chapter of 1 Timothy.

Chapter 2 and the beginning of chapter 3 are read Tuesday and Wednesday. The concern of these chapters is to provide guidelines for leading the Christian life. Obedience to authority was a concern for a young church trying to get along with the powers of the world.

The mood and message of Advent shifts this last week. From judgment we turn to promise. Galatians 3 calls for Christians to live by faith rather than rely on works of the Law. The Law of the old covenant only helps us to recognize our sinfulness; it does not bring salvation. In Christ we become heirs of God.

On Christmas Eve we read about the significance of our celebration: "But when the time had fully come, God sent forth his Son, born of woman, born under the law, to redeem those who were under the law, so that we might receive adoption as sons (and daughters)" (Gal 3:4-5). On Christmas Eve we read another hymn embedded in scripture, Philippians 2:5-11: "Though he was in the form of God, did not count equality with God a thing to be grasped, but emptied himself, taking the form of a servant, being born in the likeness of man" (Phil 2:6-7).

The Gospel readings:

Our gospel readings move us right into the celebration of Christmas with the reading of Luke's account of the events leading up to Jesus' birth. Mary's song, the Magnificat, read Wednesday, speaks about the radical nature of God's transforming action in history, made known through Jesus: "he has put down the mighty from their throne, and exalted those of low degree; he has filled the hungry with good things, and the rich he has sent empty away" (Luke 1:52-53). God's kingdom means a reversal and a transformation of the present order, and the church is to participate in that transformation. The opening chapter of Matthew can be read instead of Luke Friday and December 24.

Christmas Day and the following week

The day of the week that Christmas falls on determines the readings we use in this season. Christmas Day has an appointed set of readings (BCP, p. 941). The three days following Christmas Day are the feast days of St. Stephen, St. John, and the Holy Innocents (BCP, p. 996). Then, on December 29, return to the daily lectionary for the week following Christmas Day (BCP, p. 941). Follow the week's readings to December 31, which is also the eve of the feast of the Holy Name.

The Old Testament readings:
All of our readings this week are appropriately great hymns of praise and thanksgiving for God's mighty acts in creation and history.

A beautiful hymn of hopeful praise from Micah is read on Christmas Day. Micah wrote at about the time the northern kingdom of Israel fell to Assyria in 721 B.C.. The prophet looks forward with longing to a day of restoration when all peoples will flock to the mountain of God (Jerusalem) and live in peace together. The beautiful line, "And they shall beat their swords into plowshares, and their spears into pruning hooks," describes the coming reign of perfect peace. From the insignificant town of Bethlehem, the home of King David, a new king will come. When a woman gives birth in that city to the coming king, then the new reign of God will begin. That king will shepherd the people for God. Though Micah was looking forward to a restoration of the Davidic kingdom and a time of prosperity for Judah, Christians quickly saw this passage as pointing to the birth of Jesus.

On the First Sunday after Christmas Day we read the account of the birth of Samuel. Hannah was barren until her prayer for a child was fulfilled with the birth of her son. She dedicated his life to God as an offering of thanksgiving, and Samuel became a great prophet who shaped the history of Israel for generations to come.

David's love for Bethlehem, the town of his birth, is recounted in a story read on December 29. His love for Bethlehem reflects our feelings for the town associated with the birth of Jesus.

The theme of God granting a child to a holy woman is picked up again on December 30. The woman is the widow of Zarephath, whose son dies. The prophet Elijah is able to restore life to the child through prayer to God, and the woman rejoices with these words: "Now I know that you are a man of God, and that the word of the Lord in your mouth is truth" (1 Kings 18:24). People would know that Jesus was truly a man of God as he brought life to those about him.

Solomon's prayer for wisdom is the text for December 31. God spoke into the mind of Solomon and promised him wisdom as well as great power.

The eve of the Holy Name is New Year's Eve in our secular calendar, but to understand the significance of the appointed readings for this day keep the naming of Jesus in mind. The prophet sees a day when God will give Israel a new name and a new blessing, and with the new name shall come a reign of wonderful peace in which, "The wolf and the lamb shall feed together. . ." (Isaiah 65:25). The "new name" for the Christian, of course, is the name of Jesus. The blessing is the new age that the birth of Jesus announces to the world.

On the actual feast of the Holy Name, we find the theme of the new name for Israel repeated in our appointed reading.

The Epistle readings:

Beautiful words from the epistles express the meaning of Jesus' birth celebrated this twelve days of Christmas. On Christmas Day we read from 1 John: "In this the love of God was made manifest among us, that God sent his only Son into the world, so that we might live through him" (1 John 4:9). On the First Sunday after Christmas Day we read an ancient creedal hymn: "He is the image of the invisible God, the first-born of all creation" (Col 1:15).

December 29 and 30 readings come from the two very short epistles, 2 John and 3 John. These epistles were probably written by the author of 1 John. The letters are brief personal notes, sent to a church tempted to compromise the gospel in the face of growing resistance and heretical teaching. The church, the "Lady" in 2 John, must hold fast to the doctrine she was first taught. Third John deals with strife within the church presided over by the writer's friend Gaius. The theme of "keeping the faith" is carried into the reading appointed for December 31. We must live with the humble reality that we are not in charge of our own destiny.

On the eve of the Holy Name we read the beautiful description of the "new heaven and the new earth" that comes with the fullness of the new age. Christ is the "Alpha and the Omega, the beginning and the end" (Rev 21:6). The names of the triumphant Christ continue to be the focus on the feast of the Holy Name. In the vision from The Book of Revelation, Christ appears on a white horse and is given names of glory and victory. Christ comes to judge the nations and the peoples. The words, ". . . he will tread the wine press of the fury of the wrath of God the Almighty" (Rev 19:15) are the inspiration for "The Battle Hymn of the Republic."

The Gospel readings:

A short reading from the Gospel of John interprets the birth of Jesus for us on Christmas Day: "He who believes in the Son has eternal life. . ." (John 3:36).

On the First Sunday after Christmas Day we read the story of Jesus' ritual purification in the Temple. The familiar and beloved "Nunc dimittis" or "Song of Simeon" is included in the reading. This ancient Christian hymn embedded in Luke's gospel is often sung at funerals and is appointed for singing or saying at Evening Prayer and Compline: "Lord, now lettest thou thy servant depart in peace. . ." (Luke 2:29).

Jesus' first miracle at a wedding in Cana of Galilee is the story read on December 29, a reminder that Jesus brings new life. He turns the common stuff of life, the water, into the joy of the reign of God, the wine. The promises of the old covenant are transformed into the words and life of Jesus the Christ.

In the Old Testament reading for December 30, we read of Elijah bringing life to the widow's son. In the gospel we read the story of Jesus bringing healing to an official's son. Christ offers life in this world and in the age to come. That same point is emphasized in the text appointed for December 31, as we read of the healing at the pool of Bethzatha, of the man who was ill for 38 years.

On the feast of the Holy Name, we read the story of Jesus' birth to Mary. Joseph names the infant Jesus in accordance with the directions of the angel.

The first week in January

The first week in January we continue to follow the numbered days of the month, rather than the days of the week. Though we call the Sundays between Christmas and Epiphany the first and second Sundays after Christmas Day, traditionally the whole 12 days between Christmas and the feast of the Epiphany (January 6) are considered the season of Christmas. The familiar carol, "The Twelve Days of Christmas," reflects this tradition.

The Old Testament readings:

This week's readings are a collection of stories and psalms that recall great moments in which God was revealed to people in Old Testament times. They help us to appreciate the ultimate revelation of God in the birth, life, death and resurrection of Jesus.

On the Second Sunday after Christmas Day we read from the apocryphal book of The Wisdom of Solomon, a book attributed to King Solomon though written many years after his death. Remember the king's prayer for wisdom that we read December 31. In the text assigned for this second Sunday, the writer reflects on that prayer and Solomon's life-long quest for wisdom. Notice that Wisdom is personified as a woman. Our reading sounds like a poem written by a man in love.

This text helps us appreciate the prologue of the Gospel of John. Christ is the Word or Wisdom of God known to men and women in the flesh of human encounter. ("In the beginning was the Word, and the Word was with God, and the Word was God.") The Wisdom that the writer of the book of The Wisdom of Solomon spoke of became a person so that the world could know God's wisdom and find life in it. In a sense, a Christian would see the words written in praise of Wisdom that we read this day as words of praise to Christ who is Wisdom incarnate.

On January 2 and 3, we read of Elijah's revelation of God on the mountain. The prophet runs from the wrath of Jezebel. In a beautifully described scene God is revealed to Elijah as a "still small voice." Jesus is our "still small voice," we recognize this

Christmas season. In Jesus we see God on our own mountain-side. We learn of God's will for us in living encounters with God revealed through Christ.

In a scene reminiscent of the crossing of the Sea of Reeds (or Red Sea), we read the story on January 4 of Joshua leading the people across the Jordan river as the waters stood still. A monument of stones was constructed at the site to recall the event for future generations.

Jonah's song of thanksgiving is the text for January 5. This is an ancient psalm of thanksgiving for deliverance that was placed on the lips of Jonah during his three days in the belly of the fish. The psalm calls forth praise from us as we celebrate our deliverance known through the birth of Jesus.

The concluding words from Isaiah prepare us for the celebration of the feast of Epiphany. Writing after our Biblical ancestors returned from exile in Babylonia, the prophet sees a time when all nations "...shall come and see my glory" (Isaiah 66:18).

The Epistle readings:

A response to Jesus is a life centered on him, we are reminded in Sunday's text: "And whatever you do, in word or deed, do everything in the name of the Lord Jesus, giving thanks to God the Father through him" (Col 3:17).

The opening versicles for Holy Baptism (BCP, p. 299) are taken directly from Ephesians 4, read on January 2: "There is one body and one spirit..." This statement echoes the creedal statement of the Jews as they recite the Shema from the Book of Deuteronomy: "Hear, O Israel: The Lord our God is one Lord, and you shall love the Lord your God with all your heart, and with all your soul, and with all your might" (Deut 6:4). The writer of Ephesians proclaims the oneness that the Christian can know through Christ. There is a complete unity in God who is the source of everything.

The text for January 2 includes a quotation from Psalm 68 which the author uses to express the full ministry of Christ: "When he ascended on high he led a host of captives, and he gave gifts to men" (Eph 4:8, paraphrase of Psalm 68:18). Though the psalm spoke of Moses ascending the mountain of Sinai to bring down the gifts of the covenant, the author of Ephesians sees the text as referring to Christ who ascended to the heavens and brought the gifts of the Spirit to Christians.

In the fifth chapter of Ephesians the writer outlines norms for Christian behavior in the home and in the world. If Christians are to witness to Christ's love in the world, then their lives must reflect that love in everything they say and do and in everything they refrain from doing.

The gifts of the Holy Spirit enable us to put off the old nature and put on the new. This results in a reorientation of our actions that are now turned toward Christ. Christians must continue to put on the "complete armor" of the risen Christ if we are to avoid the temptations, the struggles and the entrapments of the present age. The priest's putting on vestments for the liturgy symbolizes the putting on of the armor of God on behalf of the whole people of God.

Our eve of Epiphany text expresses Paul's vision that all the gentile nations will praise God. Matthew's description of the coming of the Magi to worship the infant Jesus expresses that same vision. The feast of the Epiphany proclaims the clear revelation of God to all peoples.

The Gospel readings:

Our focus for Sunday and January 2 and 3 is the sixth chapter of the Gospel of John, which tells of the feeding of the 5,000 and then offers a poetic commentary on its meaning. The event for the writer of John has definite eucharistic overtones. Though the lectionary text for Sunday stops at John 6:47, read on to John 6:59 to get a full sense of the chapter. John 6 provides a sacramental statement of the Eucharist. Read it with The Book of Common Prayer open beside your Bible, comparing the great thanksgiving of the Eucharist with the words of the Gospel of John. (See BCP pp. 362-363, 368-375.) We can know today the living presence of God revealed in Eucharist and in daily encounters with Christ. The texts from the Old Testament and gospel

26

are related in theme. Elijah was fed by an angel as he fled from Jezebel. He "saw" God on the mountain. Jesus feeds the crowd and they "see" God revealed through Jesus on the hillside.

In the text assigned for January 4, Jesus anoints a blind man's eyes with his spit and the man can see. Seeing leads the man to believe in Jesus: " 'Do you believe in the Son of man?' He answered, 'And who is he, sir, that I may believe in him?' Jesus said to him, 'You have seen him, and it is he who speaks to you.' He said, 'Lord, I believe.' " At this Christmas time we, too, have seen "the Son of man." At the feast of Epiphany we recognize that his Son has also been revealed to the whole world. Our response must be the response of the one who can see: "Lord, I believe."

The signs of Jesus' power that led people to put their faith in him are recalled in our readings this week. On January 5, we read of the raising of Lazarus, a sign that pointed to Jesus' resurrection.

The Epiphany and following

We follow calendar dates for one more week. The length of this week varies according to when the first Sunday after the Epiphany falls.

The word, "epiphany," comes from the Greek word meaning "to show forth" or "to reveal." The word was used in Jesus' time to describe the appearance of a monarch before the people: "The king made his epiphany last week and talked about his foreign policies to the assembled people." In an epiphany, the ruler would express his ideas and expectations to the people. We say that Jesus was an epiphany of God in much the same sense. Moreover, the church is called to be a continuing epiphany to the world in every new generation.

The Old Testament and Gospel readings:

The Old Testament readings this week are selections from a variety of books that reflect the Epiphany themes and support the appointed gospel readings for each day. On the feast of the Epiphany we read the second servant song from the prophet Isaiah. The servant of God is called forth to reveal God's glory to the nations. Though the poetic description of the servant sounds like an individual person will be called forth, many scholars feel that the poet was referring to the role of the whole nation. In any case, as the church reflected on Jesus' life they quickly associated him with the servant songs of Isaiah. Certainly the role of Jesus as the epiphany of God is beautifully stated in the reading. The gospel reading from Matthew connects Jesus with this suffering servant figure from Isaiah.

The Old Testament reading for January 7, matches the gospel reading about Jesus as the bread of life. A similar relationship between the Old Testament reading and the gospel in the January 8 reading links the theme of God quenching the thirst of the people. Jesus is living water: "If any one thirst, let him come to me and drink" (John 7:37). In the Old Testament reading, God leads Moses and the people to water in the wilderness.

In the Old Testament and gospel readings for January 9, the

theme is recognizing God in Christ as the salvation of all peoples. Isaiah's poem calls for the nations to recognize God's presence in Israel. All nations should come and "bow down to you" (Isaiah 45:14). The gods of other nations are nothing, the poet says. The God who calls Israel as a witness to the world is a God of power. God is revealed to Israel as one who acts in both creation and in history. "I am the Lord and there is no other." In the gospel, Jesus says, "I am the light of the world; he who follows me will not walk in darkness, but will have the light of life" (John 8:12).

Jesus as the Good Shepherd is the focus for January 10. In the first reading, the prophet condemns the leadership of Judah for they have let the sheep scatter. God will raise up a new shepherd to bring the people back, the prophet promises. In the gospel Jesus proclaims himself as the Good Shepherd.

God's ways are contrasted with the ways of women and men in the Old Testament reading for January 11: "For as the heavens are higher than the earth, so are my ways higher than your ways and my thoughts than your thoughts" (Isaiah 55:9). That "way" of God is the way of Jesus the Christ, we learn from the gospel readings: "I am the way, the truth, and the life; no one comes to the Father, but by me" (John 14:6).

The January 12 Old Testament reading is somewhat obscure. We come into the midst of a scene in which old Jacob is blessing his twelve sons as he is about to die in Egypt. Judah receives his special blessing. Jacob speaks of a time when Judah shall be the leader of all the tribes. These poetic blessings originated from a later time in Israel's history. They actually reflect on what had already happened to the various tribes. Some scholars see this passage as one pointing to a future messiah who will come forth from the tribe of Judah. The last two verses of the assigned text envision a time of unbelievable prosperity. The grape vines will be thick and healthy. The king will be able to wash his clothes in wine. The vine metaphor is carried over into the gospel reading. Jesus is the vine. He is the one who is the Messiah that all nations look to. Apart from the vine we can do nothing.

On the eve of the First Sunday after the Epiphany we read from Isaiah again: "The Spirit of the Lord God is upon me, because the Lord has anointed me." These were the words Jesus quoted when he first stood up in the synagogue of his home town to preach (Luke 4:18-19). This passage is appropriate for this evening because tomorrow the church recalls the baptism of Jesus. As we remember Jesus' baptism by John in the Jordan we are called to renew our own baptismal vows which reflect the calling stated in Isaiah: "Will you strive for justice and peace among all people, and respect the dignity of every human being?" (BCP, p. 305).

The Epistle readings:

Paul's letter to the Colossians is our focus this week. How quickly the true nature of the gospel as shared by Paul became distorted by the popular ideas of the day! Colossians, written by Paul to people he had never met, urged them back to the true gospel.

Prison was Paul's environment when he wrote this letter, either at Ephesus or Rome. Writing to virtual strangers, Paul must introduce himself. Their evangelist had been Paul's "beloved fellow servant," Epaphras. Though the church of Colossae had heard the true gospel, they had soon succumbed to the influence of the religious beliefs of their neighbors. It was not Christ who controlled nature and their destiny, they were being told. Angels and mystical powers waged warfare against the believer. One must appease those angelic powers by elaborate ritual and constant seeking after the mysteries of the unseen powers. Thus a whole level of intermediaries lay between a people and God, intermediaries who must be placated and satisfied. The Christianity revealed by Epaphras soon was replaced by a Christianity that promised the secret knowledge one needed to relate to the angelic powers.

This concern for angelic or heavenly cooperation is still an issue in our society today, with anxious glances at our horoscope and careful rituals performed to placate fate. It was against this false theology that Paul wrote so passionately from his prison confinement. The January 8 reading is a creedal statement reminding the Christians of Colossae once again of the complete and utter preeminence of the risen Christ. There can be no intermediaries between the faithful and their risen Savior. It was into an eternal relationship with this Christ that the Christians were baptized. The only mystery they need concern themselves with is the mystery of Christ, and that was a mystery revealed at baptism. In Christ, the Word of God became fully known: ". . .the mystery hidden for ages and generations but now made manifest to his saints" (Col 1:26).

The theology of baptism is made clear in the January 10 reading: ". . .you were buried with him in baptism, in which you were also raised with him through faith in the working of God who raised him from the dead" (Col 2:12). Having been raised with Christ, let us keep our minds on Christ, Paul urged his readers.

The subject and feeling of the letter shifts in the January 11 reading. Paul wrote about the practical applications of the faith to Christian life. Echoes of the well-known poem of love in 1 Corinthians 13 are heard: "And above all these put on love, which binds everything together in perfect harmony" (Col 3:14).

The reading for Monday refers to family relationships: "Wives, be subject to your husbands, as is fitting in the Lord" (Col 3:18). If we are going to quote that verse to support the idea of a patriarchal family system, we must also include Paul's admonitions a few verses on: "Slaves, obey in everything those who are your earthly masters. . .Whatever your task, work heartily, as serving the Lord and not men. . ." (Col 3:22-23). Paul's words cannot be applied literally to social and ethical situations facing us today. He wrote to a particular people in a particular time.

On the eve of the First Sunday after the Epiphany we read a selection from Galatians that picks up the baptismal focus of tomorrow's liturgy.

The week of 1 Epiphany

The Old Testament readings:

Following a historic pattern of reading scripture, we begin the study of the Book of Genesis this week, a study that will take us through the week of 6 Epiphany. During Lent we will pick up our reading of Genesis again and continue reading through the Torah (first five books of the Old Testament) and historic books until we reach the Book of Judges in mid-August. In the coming weeks we will read the great stories of Israel's history as well as the stories that framed the nation's understanding of who they were as God's people.

The history of Israel begins with the call of Moses and with the Exodus. The Genesis stories set the stage. When the Hebrew people reached the land of the Canaanites they found a people with a rich tradition of mythic stories that explained the origins of the people, the roots of ritual customs and the explanation of natural phenomena. Our biblical ancestors gradually absorbed those stories and shaped them to reflect their theological understanding. The Hebrews brought with them from Egypt and the wilderness their own ancestral stories which they wove into the stories adapted from the Canaanites. The Hebrew stories helped explain the origins of the twelve tribes and some tribal traits. The stories we read in Genesis are mythic. "Myths. . .explain the unexplainable and establish for a society the basis for understanding origins, codes of morality, and life values. They tend to be the glue that holds a society together; they give the people a feeling of common origins a common understanding of life." *(Sharing our Biblical Story,* Joseph P. Russell, Winston Press, 1979, p. 11).

Genesis is a book of beginnings, which is what the name means. These stories have helped give a sense of identity not only to the ancient Hebrews, but to both Jews and Christians today.

We begin with "In the beginning God created. . ." Tuesday we read a second creation story. Compare the two accounts and note their differences. The second is actually the earlier. Though we usually think of the man being created first, some scholars hold that the word usually translated "man" (adam) could be translated "living creature" or "human being". Following that understanding Eve is one who completes or fulfills the first living creature. Part of the point of this ancient story is that a person becomes whole in relationship to another.

We read the account of "the fall" on Tuesday. Adam and Eve reach for the fruit of the trees reserved for the gods. They reach beyond their "dustness" to become more than human. They want to know as the gods know. We, too, make decisions reserved for God as we destroy the earth, create weapons of utter devastation, act as if our nation was ultimate. The ancient mythic stories treat contemporary situations. We find ourselves in them. Notice as you read Genesis that God curses only the serpent. God simply describes the struggle that man and woman bring upon themselves as a result of their striving to become like the gods. The very striving for procreation in field and in family brings pain and frustration. Unfortunately, this story has been used to denigrate women, but man and woman were both involved in taking the fruit. Both suffered as they broke trust with one another, with the fruit of the garden and with God.

The human capacity for hatred, jealousy and violence is described vividly in the story of Cain and Abel read on Wednesday. The origins of various tribes and nations lie behind the stories of births and naming that we read on Thursday.

We can see the pre-Hebrew nature of some of these stories in Friday's strange reading of the "sons of the gods" marrying the "daughters of men." The ancient story simply described the origins of a tribe of people who seemed to be larger and stronger than other tribes. The Hebrews shaped the story in such a way that it illustrated the growing disharmony in God's creation. The story sets the stage for the account of the flood that we begin reading on Saturday.

The Epistle readings:
We spend the next four and a half weeks in the Epistle to the Hebrews. This writing is more an exhortation or sermon

33

than a letter. Written late in the first century, it was addressed to a church suffering from terrible persecution, a church that could easily lose faith if another wave of persecution were to hit. Though the unknown writer of the epistle was apparently addressing gentile Christians living in Rome, he used the language of the Temple sacrificial system to make some of his major points.

Hebrews opens with these magnificent words: "In many and various ways, God spoke of old to our fathers by the prophets; but in these last days he has spoken to us by a Son, whom he appointed the heir of all things, through whom also he created the world" (Heb 1:1-2). Jesus is the fullness of the revelation of God, a suitable note to crown this epiphany theme. Extensive quotations from the psalms are used by the writer of Hebrews to build his case that Jesus is a higher order of being even than the angels and certainly than any prophet who went before him: "He reflects the glory of God and bears the very stamp of his nature. . ." (Heb 1:3). Jesus became fully man, one who lived a life "lower than the angels," and yet he was far greater than the angels. But, if he was to deliver people from their bondage and lead them to glory, then he must fully identify with their human condition. He must share in their sufferings if he was to redeem their sufferings and turn evil to good.

The author of Hebrews compares Jesus to the high priest who served in the Temple of Jerusalem. The high priest could represent the people before God because he shared all their struggles with sin. He was not aloof from the people's hurts and needs. Jesus, too, was fully human. He shared all our human sufferings as well as our joys: "For because he himself has suffered and been tempted, he is able to help those who are tempted" (Heb 2:18, Wednesday's lection). The author inserts frequent quotations from the psalms and the prophets familiar to first and second century readers.

Moses was considered the father of the house for he had led the Hebrews out of Egypt. But Jesus is far greater in that household than Moses: "Yet Jesus has been counted worthy of as much more glory than Moses as the builder of a house has more honor than the house" (Heb 3:3, Thursday). Christ is the heir of God; Moses is only the servant.

Thursday's reading ends with a quotation from Psalm 95 that reminded the Jewish people that their ancestors' unfaithfulness had resulted in their wandering in the wilderness for a generation. The wilderness testing needs to be seen as a grim reminder to the Christian church in its time of severe testing in persecution, the writer says.

With Saturday's reading (Heb 4:1-13) the author shifts from the image of wilderness wandering to the metaphor of the Sabbath rest. He picks up this metaphor from the closing words of Psalm 95 that he quoted in Thursday's reading. The rest is the promised rest of the Sabbath decreed by God at creation (Gen 2:2). The people's Sabbath rest will come ultimately as they enter with complete faith into God's promise.

The Gospel readings:

Though John followed the pattern of the synoptic gospels (Matthew, Mark and Luke) in recording the events of Jesus' life, death and resurrection, he departed radically from the gospel format in that his main interest was in giving the reader a theological interpretation of those events rather than in simply proclaiming them. John assumed that his readers knew what Jesus had said and done.

John used poetry, metaphor and symbolic language to write his theological statement of the Christ. When dealing with ultimate mystery, one must turn to these means to express the fullness of life that we can only begin to touch. As you read the long and intricate speeches of Jesus in this gospel, realize that you are reading beautiful poetry that leads the Christian to an understanding of what stands behind the words and actions of Jesus.

The opening words of John serve as a beautiful overture to his whole work. It sets forth the overriding theme and message of the gospel. The Word, or Wisdom, of God that has existed from creation came to men and women in the flesh of the man, Jesus. The word and revelation of God that reaches out to eternity to touch men and women took on flesh, became incarnate, so that people could know God intimately and personally. This is the overture that is played so beautifully at the beginning of John's gospel and at the beginning of our week together. Later in the gospel the powerful news is carried further. Through the Holy Spirit, the incarnate (in the flesh) experience of God continues, for God comes to each succeeding generation "in the flesh" of human encounter to touch men and women personally with continuing revelation. God still dwells with us!

John the Baptist pointed beyond himself to Jesus, and at least two of John's disciples turned from John to Jesus. One of those disciples was the brother of Simon Peter. The gospel according to John often differs in its account of events from the synoptic gospels. Matthew, Mark and Luke reported that Jesus called Peter as his disciple as he saw him at his fishing boat. In the Gospel of John, however, it was Peter's brother who brought Peter to see Jesus. John may have inherited different traditions about Jesus and he may have altered some stories to express his theological concerns.

The term "lamb of God," appears in Wednesday's lection. The title comes out of the Temple ritual:

> Exodus 12 directs that an unblemished lamb be slaughtered at the Passover and consumed by the people. Lambs were also offered in sacrifice at other festival days at the Temple. The offering of an innocent lamb at Passover was seen as a way of becoming at-one with God again after the separation that the people had caused by their sinfulness. The sacrifice of the Paschal or Passover Lamb restored the people to God. The Passover was a pilgrim festival; persons came from all over the nation to share this feast in Jerusalem. They would enter the city and then go to the Temple, where they would often buy a lamb from the sellers at the Temple grounds. The lamb was then offered in sacrifice. After the blood was sprinkled on the altar, the people would take the meat to their rented rooms, where it would be cooked and eaten as a part of the Passover meal....

The disciples came to realize that Jesus was the true Paschal Lamb that takes away the sins of the people by the forgiving love of God that he showed forth from the cross and at the resurrection (Joseph P. Russell, *Sharing Our Biblical Story* Minneapolis, Minn. Winston Press, 1979, pp. 151-152).

The wedding in Cana in Galilee is a symbolic narrative. To know and accept the Christ is to be purified and begin a new life. The water of the old covenant becomes the finest wine of the new covenant. That point is repeated in Saturday's reading when Jesus cleanses the Temple. The Temple must be purified, signifying the new life in Christ. The risen body of Christ, which is the church, will become the meeting place of men, women and God, rather than the Temple in Jerusalem.

The week of 2 Epiphany

The Old Testament readings:

The story of Noah and the flood begun Saturday is continued through Wednesday. God has cleansed the earth and begins again with a remnant. A part of this story is read at the beginning of Lent in year B in the Sunday eucharistic lectionary. It provides a metaphor to help us understand the nature of baptism. We too are "saved out of the waters" so that we can be a new people living in covenant with God. The first covenant between God and the human race was established with Noah, this ancient story tells us. God will not destroy the earth again. The rainbow is God's war bow hung up to announce peace.

We leave Noah and his sons Wednesday, but not before we learn of the cursing of Canaan after Ham—Canaan's father—sees Noah lying naked in drunken stupor. People hearing the story in ancient times would have associated nakedness with a sexual act between Ham and his father or perhaps between Ham and his mother. In any case, he stepped beyond the bounds of his relationship and his son, Canaan, is cursed. Ham was considered the patriarch of the Canaanites and serves as the mythic explanation of Israel's continuing struggle with this "cursed" people. Beginning with verse 24, Canaan appears to be the son of Noah rather than of Ham.

The familiar story of the tower of Babel is read Thursday. Here is an explanation for the variety of languages. Notice the recurring theme in these stories. Men and women strive to be more than they are. They want to "become like the gods." This results in punishment. Their plans are frustrated. The description of everyone understanding each other in the second chapter of Acts is a reversal of the Babel story. Human sinfulness caused confusion; the Holy Spirit brings reconciliation. Peoples are united again as God intends.

Abram and Sarai—later to be named Abraham and Sarah—are introduced on Friday with their call to leave the land they knew for a new country that God would show them. The stories about building altars at specific points was a way of establishing future claims on this land. As Abraham and Sarah found places of Canaanite worship they dedicated them to the God who had called them forth into this new land.

We end the week on a strange note. Abram tries to pass Sarai off as his sister to save his own life as they journey to Egypt. The ethics of the story are not the important point here, but rather the beauty of Israel's foremother Sarai and God's special love for her and her husband made the story an important one for the Hebrews.

The Epistle readings:

We ended our reading in Hebrews last week with stern words of warning. But these words lead to a magnificent summary of the author's points made thus far:

> Since then we have a great high priest who has passed through the heavens, Jesus, the Son of God, let us hold fast our confession. For we have not a high priest who is unable to symphathize with our weaknesses, but one who in every respect has been tempted as we are, yet without sinning. Let us then with confidence draw near to the throne of grace, that we may receive mercy and find grace to help in time of need (Heb 4:14-16).

Monday's lection closes with the statement that Jesus is a priest "after the order of Melchizedek" (Heb 5:6). This brief statement refers to Genesis 14:18-19: "And Melchizedek king of Salem brought out bread and wine; he was priest of God Most High. And he blessed (Abram)..." Since this priest and king of Salem blessed Israel's great ancestor, obviously Melchizedek represented a higher order than the priests of the temple who traced their lineage through the Levitical house of Aaron, the brother of Moses. Christ, being of that higher order of Melchizedek, takes precedence over the Temple priests. And because of his complete identification with the suffering of all people, he is the perfect high priest.

Strong words of warning that had a deep influence on the primitive church greet us with Wednesday's reading (Heb 6:1-12). One who accepts Christ and then falls away from the faith cannot hope to be restored. It's as if they have crucified Christ all over again. These words were taken literally by the church in some cases, and persons were driven out of the church. "Keep the faith," was the writer's command, even in the face of the worst persecution.

Melchizedek is mentioned also in Psalm 110:4. Melchizedek must represent a higher order of priests than the Levites, a priest forever, according to Psalm 110. "Forever" because Genesis does not mention Melchizedek's family ties. The writer of Hebrews assumed that he must have lived beyond the bounds of history and time. It is this order of Melchizedek that lays the groundwork for understanding Jesus' role as great high priest.

Unlike the priests of the Temple, Jesus does not need to make continual sacrifices year after year, for Jesus made a perfect sacrifice once and for all. "Consequently, he is able for all time to save those who draw near to God through him, since he always lives to make intercession for them" (Heb 7:25). The writer of Hebrews understood life in the world to come. The old covenant made with Moses on the mountain was imperfect. The prophets of old had known that. Jeremiah spoke of the new covenant written on the hearts of the people.

The Gospel readings:
Some familiar passages from the Gospel of John will be read this week as we continue our reading in the Fourth Gospel.

On Monday we read of a rather strange conversation between Jesus and Nicodemus, held "by night" to denote both the need for secrecy and as a symbol of coming out of darkness into light. We see here a pattern in John's writing: Jesus talks with someone at a metaphorical level. The person hears Jesus' words at the literal level and fails to understand. The gospel writer then has Jesus explain the metaphor in an extended theological discourse. This is the Fourth Gospel writer's method of expressing, in poetic terms, the theology of Christ's ministry in the world.

Notice on Thursday and Friday this same pattern is followed as Jesus encounters the Samaritan woman at the well. The living water Jesus refers to is not indoor plumbing as the woman imagines, but a relationship with God revealed through Jesus Christ!

The week of 3 Epiphany

The Old Testament readings:

Israel's claim to the land of Canaan is laid out in the travels of Abram and Sarai. They are to "look out and see" the land that God is giving them. Ancient stories of battle and intrigue are woven into the story of Abram and Sarai in Monday's reading. The narrative has little relationship to the rest of the story except that it does bring us a brief picture of Melchizedek, king of Salem, blessing Abram after the battle. Since Salem is another name for Jerusalem, his origin is significant for Israel's future. The writer of the Letter to the Hebrews saw Jesus as a priest of the order of Melchizedek. Incidentally, the Mormons see themselves as the descendants of Melchizedek.

Tuesday's reading provides us with a fascinating ritual of contract that must have been prevalent in the Middle East in ancient times. Animals and birds were cut in half and the two parties to the contract walked between the halves as a way of sealing their contract. In this case, God walks with Abram in the form of the "smoking fire pot and flaming torch."

The description of Sarai's treatment of her slave girl Hagar seems harsh and cruel as we read the account on Wednesday, but remember that we are not dealing with history here but rather with stories of origins. Ishmael's descendants were the wandering nomads or Bedouins who roamed the Middle East in biblical times. This story was told to explain their wandering nature. They shall "dwell over against all his kinsmen" (Gen 16:12).

Thursday's reading is an important one. Here God makes covenant with Abraham—a new name—and with his descendants. Sarai is now Sarah, a mark of their changed relationship and role. Circumcision is to be the mark of the covenant for all times. Abraham grows more anxious as his years increase. How could God talk of blessing when he and Sarah had no children, he asked God?

At the tender age of 99, Abraham is told that Sarah will have a son. Abraham responds to this announcement by falling on his face with laughter. It is Sarah's turn to laugh on Saturday when she hears the stranger outside her tent announce her imminent pregnancy. God obviously has a sense of humor. Their child is to be called Isaac, meaning joy or laughter! On this joyful note we end our reading in the Old Testament for the week.

The Epistle readings:

The tabernacle in the wilderness, and the Temple in Jerusalem were mere shadows of the heavenly temple. Jesus is the true High Priest of that heavenly temple, a ministry far superior to any priestly ministry in the earthly Temple.

The writer paraphrases Jeremiah's words about a new covenant that will come written on the hearts of the people. Jeremiah 31:31-34 is the source of inspiration for Hebrews 8:8-12. This is one of the many places where the writer turns to the Old Testament to make a case for Jesus' role in salvation history.

Tuesday's reading continues the comparison of the imperfect sacrifices of the Temple priests with the perfect sacrifice of Christ. We get a good description of Temple worship in Jesus' time.

The comparison of Jesus' perfect sacrifice on the cross with the priest's continuing sacrifice in the present Temple ritual leads the writer to think about a will or testament one leaves to an heir granting property and money. Before a will can take effect there must be a death. The death under the old will or testament was marked by sprinkled blood of animals. Midweek we learn that we are the heirs under a new will or testament, sealed with the blood of Christ.

Christ has actually appeared in the heavenly sanctuary on our behalf. The only direct reference to the second coming of Christ is found at the conclusion of Wednesday's reading: ". . .so Christ, having been offered once to bear the sins of many, will appear a second time, not to deal with sin but to save those who are eagerly waiting for him" (Heb 9:28).

Thursday's and Friday's readings continue the comparison between Christ's offering as the perfect priest and the imperfect offerings of Temple priests. The writer closes his argument with a call to faithfulness and evangelical fervor. The coming day is drawing close; do not lose heart after facing the initial trials of your faith, the author urges. The encouragements come with grim warning. If there is punishment for unfaithfulness under the old covenant that was sealed by the blood of animals, think how much more severe the judgment will be under the new covenant with the blood of Christ.

The Gospel readings:

The cure of the nobleman's son is the second of John's seven signs. Each sign becomes a further indication of Jesus' nature. To know Jesus is to experience eternal life, we read in John 17:3, and that life was happening as people grew to know Jesus in the signs of his love and power.

The third sign is the cure of the sick man at the Pool of Bethesda, read on Tuesday. Notice again the pattern of dialogue that grows out of the healing act. For a clearer understanding of the Gospel of John, read the discourses of Jesus as poetic statements of theology, rather than as actual speeches of Jesus. To appreciate the Fourth Gospel, we must appreciate the power of poetry and metaphor in expressing deep, unexplainable truth.

Wednesday's and Thursday's readings are John's interpretation of the healing at the Pool of Bethesda. Read this as a theological discourse on the relationship between Jesus and God the Father. God's life-giving power is revealed through Jesus. To listen to the Son is to hear the Father. To accept Jesus as the Son of God is to receive the eternal life offered by God the Father. Jesus is the source of life because God the Father is the ultimate source of life (v. 26). To reject Jesus is to reject God. These words of judgment close the discourse aimed at those who doubted the authority of the healing act they had just witnessed.

The balance of this week begins an extended reflection on the metaphor of Jesus as the bread of life. Friday's reading tells the story of the feeding of the five thousand. This scene is followed by the account of Jesus walking on the water, which sets the stage for an extended discourse on the meaning of Jesus' act of feeding that we will read next week.

The week of 4 Epiphany

The Old Testament readings:

From an announcement of imminent birth on Saturday, we move to an announcement of an imminent death with Sunday's reading. Sodom and Gomorrah are to be destroyed by the strangers (God) because of the evil being practiced. Abraham intercedes for the just people who may live there. The bargaining provides an amusing scene. "How about fifty people. Will you destroy the city if there are fifty just people there...how about forty-five just people...think about forty people...would you believe ten people? Will you destroy the city if there are ten just people there?" In this mythic story we are introduced to Abraham's role as intercessor before God, a role we all assume as God's people. And we begin to see more of God's mercy evidenced in the story. The God of Israel shows more mercy than the gods of other peoples.

Abraham's nephew Lot settled with his family in the evil city. His just actions are shown in strong contrast to his neighbors'. He invites strangers into his home and then stands before his door to protect them from a mob. He offers to send his daughters out to the men if they will leave his male guests alone. This shocking offer shows us in terrifying terms the place of daughters in the ancient household, but the audiences of the time would probably have been more struck by the extent to which Lot was willing to go to protect guests in his home.

Genesis 19:26 gives us an example of how myths were used to explain the source of natural phenomena. Lot's wife looked back at the burning city and was turned into a pillar of salt for punishment. That would have been the story parents told their children as they pointed out the human shape of a pillar of salt that was well-known in the area.

You may feel as if you are reading over familiar ground this week, for it was just last week that we read of the expulsion of Hagar and her son Ishmael. We have duplicate accounts of this expulsion woven together by the editors who fit the Torah together in final form. The first account of the expulsion came before Ishmael's birth while this one comes afterward when Sarah becomes jealous at the thought of her son playing with Hagar's son. Abraham is caught in the middle, but a word from God allows him to send Hagar off knowing that she and his son will be provided for. St. Paul uses Hagar and Sarah as metaphors for life under the gospel as compared to life under the old Law. As noted last week, Ishmael was considered the patriarch of the wandering nomads who lived to the south of the land of Canaan.

Midweek we encounter the story of Abraham's and Sarah's test. Abraham is told by God that he must sacrifice his own son as an act of faith. Father and son walk up the mountain for the sacrifice and Isaac wonders where the sacrificial animal is. We read this text at the Eucharist during Lent in year B. Christians have seen the story as an event pointing toward the sacrifice of God's only Son on the cross. Abraham's obedience showed the extent of his faith.

Abraham's faith was tested when he believed God's promise of a son who would carry his line into the future. "And he believed the Lord; and he reckoned it to him as righteousness" (Gen 15:6). Here Abraham's faith is tested to the fullest extent. Some scholars see in this story a call to the Hebrews to end the sacrificial system of their Canaanite neighbors that sometimes called for the sacrifice of the first son. St. Paul quoted this line in Romans 4:3 as proof that we earn our righteousness not by works but by faith in God's grace and mercy.

In Thursday's text we read the interesting account of Abraham's bargaining for a burial place at Sarah's death. He insists on paying for the burial place. This will establish rights for him and his descendants in the land. Notice that the deal is consummated at the town gate in the hearing of the people. The town gate served as the courthouse in ancient cities. Here disputes were settled by the elders, contracts were entered into and cases were heard.

As old Abraham prepares for his death he is determined that his son Isaac will marry someone from his own family rather than a Canaanite woman. His chief servant swears to Abraham that he will find a proper bride for Isaac. He seals his oath by putting his hand on Abraham's genitals ("Put your hand under my thigh." Gen 24:2) an ancient custom of the time. What follows in Friday's and Saturday's readings is a description of the servant's quest for a wife, told in a traditional style that will become more familiar as the Torah unfolds. The future wife is beautiful. She comes to a well where a test of word or strength is carried out and then the servant or suitor is invited to visit the woman's home where he is lavishly welcomed. Watch for this pattern in the coming weeks.

The Epistle readings:

Hebrews, chapter 11, is a beautiful reminder that the great men and women of the Old Testament lived in faith for a promise that they never saw fulfilled. (Incidentally, verses 8-16 are assigned for reading on Independence Day. Notice how appropriate the whole section is to our nation's history.) The promise that our Old Testament ancestors did not live to see is Jesus Christ. The lection for Thursday ends with a vivid reminder that we must not "lose sight of Jesus." We must live in faith, too, for the final kingdom that Christ ushered in still remains to be completed. We live in faith that Jesus ". . . has taken his place at the right of God's throne" (Heb 12:2).

After listing the great ancestors who kept the faith in the past, the writer urges the Christians to express their own faith in the yet unseen promises of God in the face of their persecution. If they can just see their pain as a discipline to strengthen them, then they should be able to bear it more easily. Their present struggles are like the struggles faced by a child disciplined by parents. By submitting to this discipline of persecution and suffering, Christians shall reap the ". . . harvest of an honest life" (Heb 12:11, NEB).

The writer alternates between words of warm encouragement and words of grim warning. Let no one become like a ". . . noxious weed growing up to poison the whole. . ." (Heb 12:15, NEB). If the Hebrews were awed as they stood before Moses at Mount Sinai, think how much more awe we feel as we stand before the living God at the heavenly Jerusalem.

The Gospel readings:

Over half this week's reading is extended discourse on the meaning of Jesus' feeding of the five thousand. Notice again the pattern of an act of Jesus followed by misunderstanding on the part of the people which calls for an extended explanation. The message is, look for the real bread of life, the bread that lasts, the bread that is Jesus, the living Christ. The discourse has definite Eucharistic overtones: ". . .he who eats my flesh and drinks my blood has eternal life. . ." (John 6:54a). Some scholars feel that John 6:51-58 was originally part of the Last Supper narrative in chapter 13 and later was moved to this position to enlarge on the theme of Jesus as the bread of life. Indeed, the whole chapter could have formed the basis for a Christian Passover celebration, using the feeding narrative and following discourse as an important part of the sacred meal (Raymond E. Brown, *Gospel of John. Anchor Bible* Garden City, New York: Doubleday and Company, 1979; p.p. 295-303). In any case, the chapter provides a beautiful sacramental statement of the Eucharist. Read it with The Book of Common Prayer open beside our Bible, comparing the Great Thanksgiving of the Eucharist with the words from the Gospel of John.
(See pp. 362-363, 368-375).

The readings for the rest of the week, taken from chapter 7, again deal with the direct relationship between Jesus and God the Father. The chapter also shows the increasing hostility toward Jesus. Though some believe, more refuse to belive despite all the signs of Jesus' power and love. Even his own brothers cannot have faith in him.

The week of 5 Epiphany

The Old Testament readings:

Young lovers meet as we begin our week in Genesis. Abraham's servant was successful. He returns with Isaac's bride and the next generation of covenant people is presented to us as husband and wife.

I mentioned the pattern of wife-finding in last week's commentary. On Monday we see another pattern that becomes familiar as we read the stories of Torah. Rebekah was barren until Isaac prayed. God provides the generative spirit of reproduction for key people in salvation history. When God intervenes to give birth, look out, for something important is going to happen. In this case, God's intervention leads to twins who begin their struggle in the womb. Esau was the patriarch of the neighboring nation of Edom. These stories would originally have been told to explain the stupidity of Israel's neighbors as compared to the brilliance of Israel's patriarchs. In Monday's account we see Esau selling his birthright for pottage. These stories are akin to ethnic jokes told today to point out supposed weaknesses of other peoples.

We read of Isaac's travels on Tuesday. The naming of places where he dug wells and established altars helped to establish claims for the land for future generations. The stories were told, in other words, as proof that the land on which the Israelites dwelt was theirs by the actions of their forefather who moved under the guidance of God.

A familiar story is read on Wednesday. Jacob steals his brother Esau's birthright by fooling his father and receiving his final blessing. This story would have delighted the ancient fireside audience. Here was yet another example of how their ancestor, Jacob, had outwitted the ancestor of the hated Edomites. The story is told with unusual detail and feeling. Old Isaac was heartsick when he found out that he had blessed the wrong son. Once a blessing was given, it could not be taken back. He did the best he could with a secondary blessing for Esau.

The stories we read in the Torah came from various sources and give different accounts of the same series of events. The process of weaving these stories together results in some anomalies. Friday we find Jacob going to his father for a blessing as he prepares to leave peacefully. The point of his departure in this second account is not fear of his brother's wrath but simply that his mother can't stand the thought that he might marry a local girl! The two accounts merge as Jacob goes off to find his wife among his uncle's people in the land of his mother.

The pattern of "boy meets girl at the well" reappears Saturday. Rachel comes down to a well to water her flocks and finds her future husband rolling back a huge stone singlehandedly. She invites him home for a warm welcome by Uncle Laban. A whole series of new adventures is about to unwind for Jacob.

The Epistle readings:

The closing chapter of Hebrews occupies our attention on Monday and Tuesday. The author gives a series of brief directives for Christian living. "Jesus Christ is the same yesterday and today and for ever," is an oft quoted verse (Heb 13:8). Monday we read that verse in its context.

We've learned a good deal about Temple sacrifice in these weeks of reading Hebrews! The writer is always looking for connections between the ritual of the old covenant and the significance of Christ's eternal ministry. In Monday's reading he ties Jesus' death outside the gates of Jerusalem to the burning of the animals outside the gates.

The writer's closing words assigned for Monday find their way into our prayer book theology expressed in our eucharistic rites: "Through him then let us continually offer up a sacrifice of praise to God, that is, the fruit of lips that acknowledge his name. Do not neglect to do good and to share what you have, for such sacrifices are pleasing to God" (Heb 13:15-16).

We complete our reading of Hebrews Tuesday and spend the balance of the week in Romans 12-14. In Hebrews we've been reading about Christ's sacrifice for us. In Romans we read Paul's words about *our* sacrifice to God.

"I appeal to you therefore, brethren, by the mercies of God, to present your bodies as a living sacrifice, holy and acceptable to God, which is your spiritual worship" (Rom 12:1). Paul's words echo the words of Hebrews. Read this opening verse with the familiar words of the eucharistic prayer from Rite I (BCP, p. 336) in mind: "And here we offer and present unto thee, O Lord, our selves, our souls and bodies, to be a reasonable, holy and living sacrifice unto thee." Each eucharistic prayer makes a statement about an offering of ourselves to God. What we offer at the Eucharist is not simply money, time or talent but our entire lives as a living sacrifice expressed in the symbols of what we have and who we are.

Friday's reading urges Christians to obey civil authorities as representing the ultimate authority of God. This passage has been used to justify blind obedience, but we must remember that Paul wrote out of his life experiences. The Roman government had protected him from the wrath of his own people. He wrote at a time when he hoped that the Christian church might somehow find legitimacy in the empire. He wrote as a citizen of Rome. Paul's words cannot be applied *carte blanche.* Throughout history Christians have stood against governments as a witness to the higher authority of God. Scripture provides many examples.

An Advent theme is set in Friday's reading. We must wake up as out of a sleep for the time of Christ's deliverance is approaching. This text is appointed for reading at the Eucharist on the first Sunday in Advent, year A. The images of Advent are beautifully set forth in the text.

Paul's major concern in Saturday's reading is for Christian unity. One is not to judge the place another Christian is in. Some Christians will follow dietary laws that others do not, but what matters is their life in God, not their outward acts of devotion. A nonjudgmental stance must inform the life of the Christian community.

The Gospel readings:

Note the increasing hostility directed against Jesus as we conclude the reading of chapter 7 Monday. You may have to do a little searching to find Tuesday's reading (John 7:53—8:11). This is the powerful story of Jesus refusing to condemn the woman caught in adultery. Since many ancient manuscripts did not incude it or placed it in different position, some Bibles will show this portion of the text as a footnote.

Wednesday we move to another metaphor about Jesus. "I am the light of the world..." we read in John 8:12. Anyone who follows Jesus will be walking in the light that comes directly from God.

Thursday through Saturday is a continuation of the dialogue Jesus has with the unbelieving Jews. Jesus' words are blunt and confrontational in the verses assigned these days. Though there is no doubt that Jesus confronted the Jews with strong words in his lifetime, the words we read here are most likely statements of the early church directed toward the Jews of the second century and written to encourage new gentile Christians. The Jews had rejected Christ and therefore, the promise was now passed on to those who could accept the signs of Jesus and become his followers. To live in the truth that Jesus brings is to be a free person, in contrast to living under the enslavement of sin.

The Jews would argue that their relationship of freedom with God was guaranteed because they were children of the Mosaic covenant. Jesus' words echo John the Baptist's statement in Matthew 32:9b: "...God is able from these stones to raise up children of Abraham." Here the writer of the Gospel of John points out that a person's relationship to God is really judged by actions. In this case the necessary action is love for Jesus and faith that he, indeed, is the Son of God.

Jesus' frequent use of the words "I am..." to identify himself was a play on the mysterious name of God revealed to Moses in Exodus 3:14: "...I am who I am...I AM has sent me to you." When Jesus said he was "I am," he meant that he himself was God. No wonder the Jews picked up stones to throw at him (John 8:59)!

The week of 6 Epiphany

The Old Testament readings:

Jacob tricked his brother. Now Jacob is the victim. His uncle Laban tricks him into working seven additional years by having him marry the veiled Leah thinking that she is Rachel. "But of course I thought you knew," the uncle says with glee. "We never marry the younger daughter first in these parts!" With the agreement to work for seven additional years, Jacob receives his favored Rachel. But she is barren. Notice the pattern? Watch for barren women for there God will act.

Sunday's reading concludes with the birth of four sons to Leah; Rueben, Simeon, Levi and Judah. These are the patriarchs of the four tribes of Israel who bore these names. Each name signifies something about the feeling of the mother.

Meanwhile Rachel remains barren. Forgetting that it is God and not husbands who bring fertility she takes things into her own hands and arranges for her husband to have sexual relations with her maid, Bilhah. This arrangement brings two sons, Dan and Naphtali. Leah is not to be outdone. She gives her maid Zilpah to Jacob, resulting in the birth of Gad and Asher. Issachar is born to Leah after she arranges for a sexual meeting with Jacob. Zebulun soon follows from Leah's womb. She desperately seeks her husband's approval, always knowing that he favors her rival. One daughter is also born to Leah. She calls her Dinah. At last, Rachel is finally able to conceive. Her first son is called Joseph. He will play a key role in the days ahead.

Laban had tricked Jacob into marrying Leah first. Now it is Jacob's turn to outwit his uncle. He manages to cross-breed Laban's flocks in such a way that he gains most of the animals from his father-in-law. Then, without telling Laban, he takes his two wives, and all his possessins and leaves. Notice in Tuesday's reading that Rachel steals her father's household gods which would have amounted to stripping him of all his power.

Wednesday's text is a true adventure story. Laban catches up with the fleeing party and accuses Jacob of stealing his household gods. Meanwhile Rachel has placed them under her in the saddlebags. Because she is having her period she has a perfect excuse for not rising from her seat to greet her father. As a result he does not find the gods and must stand by while his son-in-law upbraids him for lack of trust. The day's reading ends with the description of the erection of a boundary marker between the land of Jacob's people and Laban's people, the Arameans. A meal becomes the sign of the covenant established at the marker just as the eucharistic meal marks the covenant between Christ and the church.

Jacob's anxiety rises as he gets closer and closer to Esau's land. Thursday's reading describes in detail the elaborate preparations that Jacob makes to appease his brother even before he meets him.

Friday's narrative is important. Jacob struggles all night with an angel who turns out to be God. Jacob is marked for life with a limp resulting from the struggle. He also gains a new name, a sure sign that God is acting in his life. He is to be called Israel, meaning one who has struggled with God. An interesting name that describes a people called forth by God and who struggle both to know God and to reject God as they seek salvation. The name applies to the biblical people. It applies to God's people today.

Rachel dies giving birth to Benjamin, the last of the twelve patriarchs to be born to Jacob and his wives. Saturday's reading establishes Bethel as a major place of worship. This is the place where Jacob had his dream when he fled from his brother. He sets up markers as a way of saying that God has acted in this spot.

The season of Epiphany varies in length according to when Easter falls in a given year. Thus the last weeks after Epiphany often drop out. Readings from the Book of Proverbs are offered during the seventh and eighth weeks after Epiphany so we don't lose too much of the continuity in our lectionary reading when Easter comes early. We will pick up our reading in Genesis the first week of Lent.

The Epistle readings:
We will be reading the First Epistle of John the next two

weeks. The epistle is a late New Testament writing, coming from the same hand, or at least the same school of writing, as the Gospel of John. The author of the epistle saw the church tempted to compromise the gospel in the face of growing resistance and heretical teaching. The epistle calls the church back to the gospel as it had been received, and it reminds the church in strong words that to follow Christ is to love and serve his people in the world.

Monday's reading has the feel of the first 18 verses of the Gospel of John. You may want to read those opening words to appreciate the place that 1 John has in the New Testament. On Tuesday you will read words that may be familiar to you, as they are a part of the comfortable words offered after the confession in Rite I of the Holy Eucharist:

"...if any one does sin, we have an advocate with the Father, Jesus Christ the righteous; and he the expiation for our sins, and not for ours only but also for the sins of the whole world" (1 John 2:1-2).

The ethical implications of the epistle as it reflects the meaning of the gospel are made clear in Tuesday's reading: "He who says he is in the light and hates his brother is in the darkness still" (1 John 2:9). We cannot claim a personal relationship with the risen Christ and hate our neighbor and brother. Remember Jesus' words in the Sermon on the Mount: "But I say to you, love your enemies and pray for those who persecute you..." (Mt 5:44a).

Those baptized into the body of Christ at Easter were annointed with oil as a part of the baptismal ritual. Christians are not to forget their annointing and what it meant, we are reminded in Thursday's reading: "...as his annointing teaches you about everything, and is true, and is no lie, just as it has taught you, abide in him" (1 John 2:27b).

Our reading from 1 John ends the week with a strong reminder of the ethical imperative inherent in the gospel. What has been handed on to us is the command to love as Christ loved—an active, vital self-giving love. If we see someone in need and do not respond, then God's love cannot be in us for all the talk of being Spirit-filled.

The Gospel readings:

On Monday and Tuesday we read of the sixth sign of Jesus, the healing of the man born blind. This healing act becomes the opportunity for the writer of the gospel to reflect on the meaning of Jesus as the "light of the world." To know Jesus and to accept him as Son of God is to see truly. We are judged if we think we can see without faith in Jesus.

On Wednesday we turn to the beautiful metaphor of Jesus as the good shepherd. Well known words of faith are found in verse 10:10b: "...I came that they may have life, and have it abundantly." The good shepherd discourse continues on Thursday and Friday. Opposition from the Jews leads to their attempt again to stone Jesus. It is significant that stoning was the penalty under Mosaic law for the sin of blasphemy. Notice how many times the Jews begin to stone Jesus; look for the words he spoke that would have led them to such an act. Jesus claimed over and over again to be one with the Father, according to the writer of John.

On Saturday we turn to the seventh and final sign of Jesus, the raising of Lazarus. The act leads to Jesus' powerful statement, "I am the resurrection..." This sign is a physical carrying out of Jesus' words in John 5:28: "...for the hour is coming when all who are in the tombs will hear his voice and come forth...." The event points to the full meaning of Jesus' life and to the presence of the risen Christ among all peoples. Technically, this is not a resurrection account. Lazarus was brought back to life in this present age, but the story serves to dramatize the theological statements the writer of John has been making in the preceeding chapters.

The week of 7 Epiphany

The Old Testament readings:
"Most of the writings of the Old Testament seek the wisdom implicit in the *story* of God's relationship with his people as a *people*. It is the wisdom of the story told by the historian, the teller of legends, the prophet, and by the priest as he recalls the story in ritualistic acts. But after returning from exile, the Jews came to appreciate a type of writing popular in other nations around them—wisdom literature. This kind of writing does not deal with the *story* and its interpretation, and it does not focus on the community of God's *people*. Rather it uses *non-narrative* forms and seeks for truth as it applies to the *individual* who wishes to live a happy life.

"The Book of Proverbs comes out of this postexilic time. Paging through it, the reader can quickly see that it is filled with short proverbs not unlike the "Confucious say" style familiar to the joke teller. But underneath these proverbial sayings is the unique Jewish understanding that the heart of all wisdom is awe and worship ("fear") of the Lord. To seek after wisdom is to seek after the Lord" (Joseph P. Russell, *Sharing our Biblical Story*, Minneapolis, Minn: Winston Press, 1979, pp. 60-61).

The readings for the next two and a half weeks are portions of the Book of Proverbs. In the opening verse of the book, which is not assigned for our reading in the lectionary, Proverbs is attributed to King Solomon. But the writing comes much later in history than Solomon's reign. His name was used because of his reputation for great wisdom.

On Monday, Tuesday, Friday and Saturday we read passages that give Wisdom a feminine personification: "She is more precious than jewels, and nothing you desire can compare with her" (Prov 3:15). In chapter 8 we read that Wisdom was created by God at creation and has been with God ever since. Wisdom is recognized as a direct gift from God. To seek Wisdom is to seek God, but Wisdom is no mere body of knowledge. Rather Wisdom is that aspect of God that seeks to inspire men and women with the knowledge of God's will for them. The pronoun, "she," gives us a personal feeling toward this aspect of God that gives wisdom to the seeker after truth. Ever since the dawn of creation Wisdom has been seeking to communicate God's wisdom to men and women, the writer of the Book of Proverbs pointed out. "The Lord created me at the beginning of his work, the first of his acts of old" (Prov 8:22). Compare that statement with the powerful poem that provides an overture for the Gospel of John: "In the beginning was the Word, and the Word was with God, and the Word was God. . ." (John 1:11). If you replace "Word" with "Wisdom" in John's prologue you get a sense of how Christ was understood by John and the primitive church. That aspect of God that reaches out to man and woman took on flesh in Jesus. Wisdom became incarnate, enfleshed, in the man Jesus. Wisdom became a person reaching out to people to bring them the nearer knowledge of God. "Jesus is the wisdom of God," Paul declared in 1 Corinthians 2:24. Christ is that aspect of God which communicates God to man and woman.

There can be no more important goal in life than the acquiring of Wisdom, we are reminded on Tuesday. Turn to 1 Kings 3:4-15 and read Solomon's prayer for Wisdom. God came to the king in a dream and promised a rich reward for Solomon, who sought wisdom above power and prestige for himself.

Much of our reading this week is framed in the wise sayings of a father handing on good advice to his son. Loose women are a major concern in this fatherly advice.

On the surface, the Book of Proverbs may not seem the most illuminating reading assigned in the daily lectionary, but if you consider the theological implications of God reaching out to men and women to reveal the creator's presence and will, these simple sayings may take on added meaning for you.

The Epistle readings:
We continue reading 1 John. Keeping the commandments of Christ is the only way of truly being his follower. We are to believe in the gospel given to the church. Jesus is the Christ, the

Son of God, and we must love in the way that he showed us in his life, suffering and death. Whoever keep these commandments "...abide in him, and he in them..." (1 John 3:24a). These words may sound familiar because they are paraphrased in the prayer of consecration from Rite I: "...that he may dwell in us, and we in him" (BCP, p. 336).

Monday's reading sets forth a standard of faith, an orthodoxy. We must believe that "Jesus the Christ has come in the flesh." This orthodox statement would set the true follower of Christ apart from those who were coming into the church with heretical doctrines that denied that Christ was both man and God.

On Tuesday we read a summary of the gospel: "God is love, and he who abides in love abides in God, and God abides in him" (1 John 4:16). These words are soon followed by the warning: "If anyone says, 'I love God,' and hates his brother, he is a liar; for he who does not love his brother whom he has seen, cannot love God whom he has not seen" (1 John 4:20).

On Wednesday our reading opens with a simple statement of faith that circulated in the early church: "Jesus is the Christ." This creed must be on the lips of the Christian just as acts of love must shape the life of the Christian. This is the praxis statement of Christian faith, the putting into action of one's beliefs. We do our faith by the way we respond to God's people in justice and in acts of love and compassion.

Christ is synonymous with life, we learn on Wednesday, for he came to overcome the world through his baptism (the water) and his death (the blood). The letter ends with strong words of forgiveness for the sinner. Notice how similar the closing words of the epistle are to the closing statements of the Gospel of John. Compare 1 John 5:13 with John 20:30-31.

On Friday we read the letter of Paul to Philemon, a personal note to a leader in the church at Colossae. It would appear that Paul was writing from Rome where he was kept under house arrest. Philemon's slave, Onesimus, had run away, but had become a close companion of Paul's during his imprisonment. Paul asks Philemon to welcome his slave back, foregoing the usual punishment for runaways. Paul hints that he would like to have Onesimus back himself, for the slave had become a comfort to Paul during the time they had been together. The letter is delightful to read. Notice the not-so-subtle pressure Paul puts on the Christan leader. A little pious arm-twisting seems appropriate to Paul as he supports his friend, Onesimus. Colossians 4:4-7 contains a reference to Onesimus' return to Colossae, incidentally.

On Saturday we begin reading the Second Letter of Paul to Timothy. I'll have comments about this epistle in next week's commentary.

The Gospel readings:

The narrative of the raising of Lazarus occupies our attention for the first three days of this week. Thursday's gospel reading leads us into a major turning point in the Gospel of John. Jesus entered Jerusalem the final time and prepared to face the death he knew awaited him. The anointing at Bethany seems a fitting preparation for that death, since bodies of those who died were anointed for their burial (John 12:7).

Palm Sunday may be in our minds as we read on Friday the account of Jesus entering Jerusalem. Saturday's reading is a beautiful statement of the meaning, not only of Jesus' death, but of our own as well: ". . .unless a grain of wheat falls into the earth and dies, it remains alone, but if it dies, it bears much fruit" (John 12:24).

The week of 8 Epiphany

The Old Testament readings:
We'll conclude our reading of the Book of Proverbs next week, so don't let the long series of wisdom sayings exhaust you. These proverbs shared by our biblical ancestors provide us with some insights about the values Jesus' ancestors held. Remember that he would have been raised on these ancient sayings. Some of them would have framed his imagery as he spoke with people. For example, Sunday's reading uses the metaphor of a great banquet held by Dame Wisdom in which she offers the fine wine of wisdom. Think about the parable of the Great Feast that Jesus told: "And again Jesus spoke to them in parables, saying, "The kingdom of heaven may be compared to a king who gave a marriage feast for his son, and sent his servants to call those who were invited. . .'" (Matt 22:1-3). The imagery of a feast becomes the setting of a parable told by Jesus to speak of the kingdom of heaven. Those invited to the feast refused the invitation to participate.

For the most part you will be reading a series of proverbs this week. You may feel as if you are opening a stack of Chinese fortune cookies by the time Saturday comes! The sayings are not so random as they may appear at first glance, however. They were grouped into several different collections of sayings by the final editors of the book.

The Epistle readings:
We began our reading in Second Timothy on Saturday. This letter is about one of the three pastoral concerns of the primitive church. Many scholars feel that though these epistles are attributed to Paul, in fact they were written by disciples of Paul at a later date. Other scholars think the pastorals are, indeed, from the hand of Paul himself, written at the time of his imprisonment in Ephesus or Rome. (Second Timothy purports to have been written from Rome). Read Acts 16:1-5 to learn of Timothy's place in Paul's ministry.

Suspicion about Paul's authorship stems from the concerns of the pastoral epistles. Paul lived with the expectation that Christ would return very soon to begin the reign of God. The pastoral epistles, on the other hand, seem to have been written at a time when Christians were beginning to realize that they had to be ready for the long haul in the present age.

With this in mind, go back to Saturday's lection and read again 1:13-14: "...guard the truth that has been entrusted to you...". Faith and truth are now equated with specific doctrine that must be treasured and guarded against the heresies of the time. Paul, on the other hand, used the word "faith" to express one's whole orientation to life. He talked about a faith in Christ that was acted out in the lives of people rather than being a body of doctrine that must be guarded.

An ancient hymn may lie embedded in Monday's reading "If we have died with him, we shall also live with him, if we endure we shall also reign with him..." (2 Tim 2:11-13). Paul's own struggles were perceived by him as a part of the suffering that would lead to the victory of Christ's resurrection. Suffering is not empty and meaningless. In Christ it is life-giving as one identifies personally with the suffering of Christ.

Notice on Wednesday the emphasis on the importance of scripture in equipping the Christian "for every good work" (2 Tim 3:17). These words remind us of the role of scripture in our lives. We read so that we may be properly equipped for every good work.

We begin reading the Epistle to the Philippians on Saturday. See my comments in next week's notes about this epistle.

The Gospel readings:

These scenes in Jerusalem offer the writer of the Gospel an opportunity to express again the theological implications of Jesus' life, death, and resurrection. Jesus is the light that comes into the world. Can we dare to choose to live in darkness when the light has come?

The last half of chapter 12 echoes the opening words of the gospel, but the words take on a new significance as we move with Jesus into his final struggle.

John's description of the Last Supper occupies our attention from Wednesday to Friday. Notice that this is a very different description of this crucial event than is found in Matthew, Mark or Luke. Here the focus is on the footwashing rather than on the bread and cup. (Remember, however, that some scholars feel John 6:51-58 may at one time have been connected with the Last Supper narrative.) Jesus performs an act of humiliation and servanthood that is meant to point ahead to his total act of humiliation on the cross for the salvation of the world. As is so often the case in John's gospel, the hearers of Jesus' word misunderstand the meaning of what he says and does. This results in a dialogue between Peter and Jesus that has baptismal overtones. One must be washed to be a part of Jesus' saving action. But beyond baptism, the washing could also refer to being "washed" in the suffering of Jesus as well. That is, the disciple must be ready to enter into the saving action of the cross. The disciple must be ready to do as Jesus did, in other words. Thus this scene is far more than a ritual act. It is a scene which calls us to a new orientation of our lives: "For I have given you an example, that you also should do as I have done to you". (John 13:15).

Judas leaves the scene in Thursday's reading. Jesus really orders Judas to do what he must do. The writer of the gospel wants to make it clear that Jesus was not trapped into dying on the cross. He managed the affair, so to speak. On Friday, we discover why he directed his own suffering and death. It is to bring glory to God; to reveal to people in every generation the power of God over sin, death and evil. Jesus will meet every destructive power and defeat it with the grace of God.

John 13:34 is the source for the term "Maundy Thursday," the Holy Week remembrance of the Last Supper. "A new commandment I give to you, that you love one another; even as I have loved you, that you also love one another." "Maundy" derives from the Latin for "commandment."

We shift Saturday from the Last Supper scene described in John 13 to the garden scene where Jesus is arrested, described in John 18. The intervening chapters are Jesus' extensive discourse that interprets the coming passion and sets the stage for understanding the resurrection. These chapters are assigned during the second week of Easter, preparing us to hear portions of the same chapters as they are read as the Gospel at the Sunday Eucharist during the later Sundays of the Easter season. We'll complete the reading of chapter 18 on Monday and Tuesday of next week.

The week of Last Epiphany

The Old Testament readings:
In this final week after Epiphany we read a potpourri of Old Testament selections that pick up the theme of transfiguration from Sunday's eucharistic lectionary readings and then shift to the penitential mood of Ash Wednesday and Lent.

Sunday's reading is from Ecclesiasticus (or Sirach) found in the Apocrypha. It is a hymn of praise to the great prophet Elijah. Those who saw Elijah are called blessed. Jesus was seen on the mountain in the company of Elijah and Moses, we hear this Sunday at the Eucharist. Those who saw Jesus are truly blessed, a fact we celebrate on the Last Sunday of Epiphany.

We return to Proverbs for our Monday and Tuesday readings. The writer asks sarcastically how one can know God's wisdom when no one has "ascended to heaven and come down" (Prov 30:4). The Christian would read this through the eyes of the gospel. Jesus revealed the wisdom of God by "coming down" and living as one of us.

Strong words of prophetic judgment greet us on Ash Wednesday, helping to set the theme and mood for the season of Lent. The prophet Amos spoke to the people of the northern kingdom in the 8th century BC. He confronted the people of that age and he confronts us today with a call to "Hate evil, and love good and establish justice in the gate. . ." On Thursday we read in Habakkuk a psalm of God's victory on behalf of the people. God shakes the very foundations of the earth and defeats the enemy for the sake of the righteous nation. Judgment and hope are balanced in this week leading to Lent.

Ezekiel holds our attention the last two days of the week. He wrote during the Babylonian exile. The words we read on Friday both comfort and confront us. A saying popular during Ezekiel's time expressed the idea that each generation was responsible for the sins of those who had gone before: "The Fathers have eaten sour grapes, and the children's teeth are set on edge" (Ezek 18:2). Not so, says Ezekiel. We do not bear the burdens of those who have gone before, but we do bear the responsibility for our own sins. Ezekiel calls the people to have a new spirit and a new heart. God does not want to see anyone die for their sinfulness. God would far rather that they turn from their wickedness and live. This week of turning-to-Lent ends with the hope expressed by Ezekiel that God's people in exile will be restored. God's glory will again be seen by other nations as they realize that God's people suffered for their sins and were then restored.

The Epistle readings:

We began Paul's letter to the church at Philippi last Saturday. For background on Paul's life among the Philippians, read Acts 16:11-40. Scholars disagree on where Paul wrote the letter. Maybe from a prison cell at Ephesus or from Rome, where he was held under house arrest for some time. Despite his imprisonment, Paul wrote with a sense of joy and gratitude for what the Philippians had done to support him and for their growing faith in God. His only concern was that he had heard there were some who were trying to convince them that they must adopt the strict ritualistic provisions of the Jews in order to be followers of Christ. Paul warned his friends to avoid such demands. Christ had brought them a new covenant. They were not to fall back into the practices of the old.

Philippians 2:6-11, read on Monday, is probably an ancient liturgical hymn or creed inserted there by Paul.

Philippians 2:12 may be familiar to you: ". . .work out your own salvation with fear and trembling," along with Philippians 3:10 which reads, "All I care for is to know Christ, to experience the power of his resurrection, and to share in his sufferings, in growing conformity with his death if only I may finally arrive at the resurrection of the dead" (NEB). Another familiar passage comes on Friday, one often used in connection with the blessing offered at the Eucharist: "And the peace of God, which passes all understanding, will keep your hearts and minds in Christ Jesus." (4:7)

The Gospel readings:

We pick up the story of Jesus' arrest and interrogations before Annas, Caiphas and Pilate on Monday and Tuesday. The lectionary is selective. We concentrate on Peter's denial, and the initial interrogation of Jesus before Pilate. Jesus' witness is to the truth of God's Word, a truth that Pilate cannot understand. We see in this scene the terrible struggle between God's truth and the world's truth, the contrast between light and darkness. The people called to live in God's truth, turn away from the Epiphany of God and choose to live in darkness instead. "The Jews" mentioned in John's gospel need to be understood as "the Christians" of every generation if this passage is to have its full impact. As we read this passage at the end of the great Epiphany season and on the eve of Ash Wednesday and Lent, we come face to face with our own turning from the light of the gospel. These passages call us to repentance.

On Ash Wednesday we read the parable of the Pharisee and the tax collector. It is the tax collector's acknowledgment of his sinfulness that makes him righteous before God. The Pharisee's pride at not being like the tax collector leaves him to be humbled before God. In early lectionaries this was the gospel lesson appointed for the Eucharist on Ash Wednesday rather than the present lectionary text that calls for clean faces in times of fasting so that we do not take pride in expressing humility.

The priest at the Eucharist remembers the mighty acts of God in history and in creation and then offers the bread and wine saying, "Sanctify them by your Holy Spirit to be for your people the Body and Blood of your Son. . ." (BCP, p. 363). John 17, read the last three days of the week, could be seen as a "consecration prayer" for the church. God's mighty acts are remembered by Jesus who then offers his disciples to be consecrated by God to be "outward and visible signs" of God's continuing action in the world.

In the Epiphany season we concentrate on how Jesus revealed God. In this prayer Jesus remembers his ministry: "I glorified thee on earth, having accomplished the work which thou gavest me to do. . ." (John 17:4). Jesus has been the ultimate epiphany of God in the world. (See introductory remarks on the Epiphany). Then Jesus prays: "As thou didst send me into the world, so I have sent them into the world and for their sake I consecrate myself, that they also may be consecrated in truth" (John 17:18-19). Now it will be the disciples who will be an epiphany of God before the world in the generations to come. The season provides a framework in which we can understand the nature of our mission to be an epiphany ourselves.

The Bible and Lent in the early Church

In the primitive church, Lent was a time of final preparation for those who were to be baptized on Easter Sunday. Three years was the normative time for a person to spend in preparation for initiation into the church. During these long months of preparation, candidates for baptism had heard the salvation story of the Hebrew scriptures, the good news as proclaimed in the gospel accounts and the theological reflections of the good news as outlined in the epistles of St. Paul and other early Christian leaders.

As their baptisms grew closer, the candidates gradually took on the Christian life style. They saw themselves as citizens of God's coming reign rather than as citizens of the Roman Empire. God's word and God's work formed in them a deepened consciousness and demanded a radical obedience. Lent was the final preparation time. Like Jesus, they spent forty days struggling with the temptations of evil and with their own fears. They took on added practices of obedience to the calling of Christ and they rehearsed, once again, the whole sweep of salvation history. Gradually, the whole Christian community began to adopt the Lenten call for obedience and to remember the salvation story. For them, Easter became a time of renewed commitment to the covenant of baptism.

The first week of Lent
Year Two

The Old Testament readings:
We have been reading the Book of Genesis since the first week in Epiphany. This week of Lent, we move into a major segment of the book. This is the story of Joseph, favored son of Jacob, dreamer and savior of Egypt and Israel. Evidence suggests that this saga could have been written as late as the time of Solomon. It provides a link between the primitive stories of Israel's origins and the Exodus of Israel from Egyptian oppression under the leadership of Moses.

The message of these closing chapters of Genesis is clear. God is at work in history and in the day-by-day affairs of men and women. "The Lord was with Joseph, and he became a successful man," is the constant refrain of the Joseph saga (Gen 39:2). Moreover, Joseph's grace flowed out to others with whom he came into contact. He was a favored son of old Jacob, but more than that, he was a favored son of God who was destined to save his family, Israel.

It is important to remember at the outset, that Joseph was the first of Rachel's two sons. Rachel had been barren for a long time before Joseph's birth. This should be clue enough that Joseph was to play a key role in salvation history. Children born of barren women are always marked for greatness in Biblical stories. Benjamin was Joseph's only full brother. Rachel died at Benjamin's birth. Little wonder, then, that old Jacob would dote on Joseph in a special way. While his older sons cared for the sheep, Joseph had a special relationship with his father, symbolized by the coat of long sleeves (in the King James Version, it is a "coat of many colors").

Joseph's dreams of power and greatness do not help him in his relationship with his brothers. They first plot murder and then decide to sell him into slavery as a chance to rid themselves of their spoiled brother. In Wednesday's readings we see two versions of the story merged into one narrative as is so often true in scripture. First, we read that the brothers will sell Joseph to the Ishmaelites. We then read that Midianite merchants took him out of the pit to sell him themselves.

We skip over chapter 38 between Wednesday and Thursday. That chapter is an independent story that has no bearing on the overall narrative. Joseph's early adventures in Egypt capture our attention for the balance of the week. Joseph is immediately successful under his first master, Potiphar, and then under his jailer. His honorable character as a man of God is established for us as we read of his refusal to have sexual relations with his master's wife.

The Epistle readings:

The Lenten epistle this year in the daily lectionary is Paul's First Letter to the Corinthians. The 18th chapter of the Acts of the Apostles provides us with a brief description of Paul's first visit to the important and thriving city. Paul spent about 18 months among the people of the city, which was no small investment of time and energy for the roving missionary apostle. No wonder he had strong feelings when he discovered that after he left Corinth, deep divisions had split the young church. While in the city of Ephesus, Paul wrote a letter back to Corinth. Unfortunately, all but a small piece of that letter is lost. We have a reference to it in First Corinthians 5:9 and we may have a fragment of it preserved, included in the body of Second Corinthians (See 2 Cor 6:14-7:1). Paul's letter elicited a response from the Corinthians. They wrote him back asking a series of questions that Paul responds to in our letter under study (See 1 Cor 7:1). First Corinthians was probably written in 55 or 56 AD.

As we begin our reading on Monday, it quickly becomes obvious why Paul wrote his letter. Though the great gift of faith in Christ has come to the Corinthian church, Paul has heard of their divisions. It appears there are actually four churches. Some call themselves Paul's people, others are Apollos' people, some belong to Cephas (another name for St. Peter) and some to Chloe. How painful those divisions must have been to Paul as he wrote that letter from so far away. The church he had left so strong in the faith of Christ was now split in competing factions, each one claiming superiority over the other.

The gospel that Paul had proclaimed in Corinth appealed mostly to the lower classes. The wealthy and powerful were caught up in their own wisdom, it would seem. They considered the cross of Christ a ridiculous doctrine to espouse. Paul wrote of the folly of the cross as it confronted the wisdom of the world. "For the foolishness of God is wiser than men, and weakness of God is stronger than men" (1 Cor 1:25). Perhaps Paul saw the working people who responded to the gospel as symbols of the weak confronting the false wisdom of the

71

wealthy and powerful of the city. Paul's statements about weakness and the folly of the cross echo Jesus' words.

The Corinthian church received the Spirit of God and not the spirit of the world, we are reminded in Wednesday's text. It is God's Spirit that explores for us the very depths of God's nature. Thus, what the Corinthians have discovered about God is not something they have gained on their own. Rather, it is a gift given through the Spirit. How can they have pride when they should have only praise and gratitude? That is the question Paul raises as he looks at the competing parties of the church. The fact that the church is divided is a clear indication that the Spirit is being rejected by the people.

Jesus had spoken about raising up a new temple after three days, a temple that was to be his body rather than a building in Jerusalem (John 2:19). The people of Corinth are reminded by Paul that they are a part of that temple. Christ must be the only foundation of that building. The "building materials" each Christian supplies for the construction of the temple will finally be tested, Paul warns. That powerful metaphor leads to a warning. "If any one destroys God's temple, God will destroy him, for God's temple is holy, and that temple you are" (1 Cor 3:16). Divisiveness in the body certainly leads to the destruction of the temple, the very body of Christ.

"This is how one should regard us, as servants of Christ and stewards of the mysteries of God" (1 Cor 4:1). The Holy Spirit has opened to Christians the mysteries of God's presence and pilgrimage toward salvation. The Christian is the steward of great mysteries. From that beautiful metaphor, Paul moves on to a defense of his own ministry among the people. God will judge how Paul exercised his stewardship. No one else, none of those other divisive factions of the church, can make the judgment on Paul. Apollos was one of the leaders of the Corinthian church whom Paul trusted. Paul had planted the seed and Apollos had watered it. Both must be humble in the knowledge that they are merely agents of the Lord's action among the people. Paul wants their example of humble stewardship and servanthood to be an example for the Corinthians.

The Gospel readings:

We begin our reading of Mark on Monday. This gospel may have been written for the church in Rome, but that remains conjecture. The Temple in Jerusalem had just been leveled by Roman armies as they crushed the last attempts of Jewish Zealots to overthrow foreign rule. Moreover, the church was undergoing presecution. Christians were scattering as conditions in Jerusalem grew worse.

In this painful historic situation, the writer of the Gospel of Mark collected the stories of Jesus that he knew and wove them into a proclamation of good news. The basic message: Have hope, for the agony of the present time is the dawning of the age of fulfillment that is coming soon. The suffering of Christ is God's way of achieving victory over evil. The battle has been won and Christ, not the evil powers of the present age, is the victor. The core of Mark's gospel is that those who keep faith in this good news will share both in the suffering and the glory of the risen Christ.

Mark loses no time getting into the message of the gospel. No birth story precedes the ministry of the Lord. John appears in the wilderness as a rustic Elijah figure to announce the new age. Jesus comes up out of the waters of his baptism to be led into the wilderness where he, unlike his ancestors in the Sinai wilderness, overcomes the temptations of evil.

The authority of Jesus to drive out evil, to teach, and to call disciples, is expressed with power in our reading for Tuesday. His presence is living witness that the reign of God has dawned.

The Jewish people at the time of Jesus, yearned for the ushering in of the messianic age. Evil would be defeated and the Lord's kingdom would triumph. This expectation of the triumphant ending of the present age of darkness, with the coming of God's kingdom, framed the hopes and expectations of the Jewish people who saw their lives torn apart by one oppressive power after another. They remembered their nation's history and the grand days of David and Solomon. They dreamed of a new David and a new kingdom. In the prophetic poetry found in the Book of Daniel, a figure is introduced in Daniel 7:13 that seems to usher in this day of God's new age: "I saw in the night visions, and behold, with the clouds of heaven there came one like a son of man, and he came to the Ancient of Days and was presented to him. . ." One of Mark's purposes in writing his gospel was to point out over and over again, that this triumphant Son of Man, who was expected at the coming of the new age was, in fact, Jesus of Nazareth. Other terms were used to describe this great figure, such as Messiah or Son of God. We see these terms used throughout the gospels.

Mark drew together all the stories he knew that proved Jesus was the expected Messiah.

Satan was the master of the present age of darkness. Evil, sickness and death were all the dominion of the kingdom of Satan. People who were mentally or physically ill were thought to be possessed by demons. They lived under the cloud of darkness. Jesus' healings and exorcisms were signs that the victory of the kingdom of light over the kingdom of darkness had begun.

Only God could forgive sins. Temple priests could accept offerings for the forgiveness of sins, but even they could not pronounce the restoration of man and woman to God. Jesus spoke as God when he stated forgiveness and healing to a paralytic lowered to him through the roof of a home. Such a statement would be blasphemy to a Jew. We cannot blame the scribes and Pharisees for their shocked response. Jesus spoke words reserved for God. The lowering and raising of this man may point ahead to the resurrection. The man was lowered as in a grave, and he was raised up as a new being in Christ.

Because Jesus acted with the authority of Messiah, he could change the laws of Torah (the first five books of the Old Testament). This is a new age that cannot be contained within the old, he pronounced. "No one sews a piece of unshrunk cloth on an old garment. . .no one puts new wine into old wineskins. . ." (Mark 2:21-22)

The second week of Lent

The Old Testament readings:

God's power is revealed in Joseph. That becomes obvious again when Joseph is able to interpret Pharaoh's strange dreams. The blindness of the state-approved scholars and wise men stands in sharp contrast to the insight of Joseph, the strange foreigner hauled out of prison to speak before the ruler. The words of St. Paul, which we read last week, come to my mind as I read of Joseph's appearance before Pharaoh. "Where is the wise man? Where is the scribe? Where is the debater of this age? Has not God made foolish the wisdom of the world?...but God chose what is foolish in the world to shame the strong, God chose what is low and despised in the world, even things that are not, to bring to nothing things that are, so that no human being might boast in the presence of God" (1 Cor 1:20, 27-28). Joseph's power to interpret Pharaoh's dreams, along with his quick insight into how Pharaoh must act in response to the dreams, brings details of Joseph's investiture as ruler over all of Egypt. Notice the signs of his new office including the giving of an Egyptian name to go with his Egyptian authority.

Joseph's earlier dream of his brothers' bowing down to him comes true as his family is forced to turn to Egypt for food in time of famine. First, all of Egypt has been ordered to bow down to Joseph with all his new powers as ruler (Gen 41-43), and then his brothers find themselves bowing down before him as they greet him seeking food relief (Gen. 42:6). Joseph recognizes his brothers but treats them roughly. The brothers fail to recognize Joseph. They suddenly find themselves under suspicion for spying by the Egyptian official. You can sense their fear at Joseph's accusation. Joseph plots a way to force the brothers to produce Benjamin who had been left behind with Jacob. One brother shall be held as hostage until Benjamin is produced on a subsequent trip. Though the brothers remain ignorant of Joseph's identity, they do sense that somehow they are paying for their earlier actions against their brother.

The story of Joseph carries more details than is usual in biblical accounts. Jacob's anguish over his sons is clearly developed in Thursday's and Friday's reading. Finally, hunger forces him to send Benjamin along with the other brothers. With foreboding, the men approach the Egyptian ruler again, but on this occasion, Joseph treats them with great kindness and generosity.

The Epistle readings:
Our reading in First Corinthians this week opens with biting words of sarcasm. The Corinthians seem to feel superior to the apostle who saved them in Christ. It is as if they have already decided that the kingdom of God has dawned for them, shutting out the very one who brought them news of the kingdom! The pain mixed with anger that Paul must have been feeling as he wrote this letter, comes across clearly as we read his words written so many years ago. The apostle Paul proclaims weakness while the Corinthians seem to parade their power. May the Corinthians take Paul and Apollos as their model and live in humbleness and expectancy rather than in pride and competitiveness. Paul warns of his impending visit. He writes in the manner of a teacher returning to class after a long absence.

On Tuesday, we move into the second major section of the letter, in which Paul addresses the problems inherent in leading the Christian life in the midst of a fallen society. He responds to the questions the Corinthians had asked him in their letter, and he speaks to situations that he is aware have arisen during his absence. For example, he has heard that a man in the church has either married or is living with his stepmother. According to Leviticus, this was strictly prohibited for Jews. Paul makes his judgment out of his studies of Torah. The penalty for such an illicit relationship was death, according to Leviticus. Paul condemns the man at least to excommunication if not to death. ". . .You are to deliver this man to Satan for the destruction of the flesh, that his spirit may be saved in the day of the Lord Jesus" (1 Cor 5:5). An interesting statement of theology: The man's death is to end in salvation at the day of the Lord. It would seem that in Paul's mind, the evils inherent in the man's body would be destroyed, allowing the spirit of the man to find salvation in the Lord. Paul's strict words of condemnation need to be read in the light of the whole gospel of Christ, a gospel of mercy and forgiveness, a gospel that speaks of one's whole being, that is body and spirit, made one in Christ, a gospel Paul himself reflects later in this very letter.

Leaven was a metaphor of evil in biblical times. All leaven is still removed from the Jewish home at the Passover as a symbol of removing evil from the home of the faithful at the holy season. But Christ is the new Passover. The Christian eats the unleavened bread of the new Passover that is Christ's death and resurrection. "Christ our Passover is sacrificed for us; therefore let us keep the feast," are words said at the Eucharist after the breaking of the bread. The origin of those words that may be familiar from the liturgy, are found in the fifth chapter of the epistle.

Evil doers are to be driven from the congregation of faithful. Our midweek text led to the practice of "shunning" among some Christian bodies over the years. Canon law and prayer book rubrics dealing with excommunication stem in part from Paul's strong directives for the church in Corinth. Paul was shocked to hear that Christians were dragging each other into pagan courts for judgment. Surely the faithful, who would themselves act as judges even of the angels at the day of the Lord, should be able to judge simple matters of ethics among themselves! Paul's surprising statement, that the church would share the responsibility for judgment at the day of the Lord, stemmed in part from the book of Daniel chapter 7, verses 9, 22 and 27. The Christian faces judgment, but the Christian also serves as fellow judge with Christ, it would seem.

The Christian's body is no longer his own. "Do you not know that your body is a temple of the Holy Spirit within you, which you have from God? You are not 'your own'; you were bought with a price. So glorify God in your body" (1 Cor 6:19-20). We are not free to do anything, as some of the Corinthians were obviously saying. We are only free to act for Christ in the world. Earlier in this letter, we learn that the whole church is the new temple of the Lord in the world. Here we are reminded that each individual Christian is to be a temple of the Lord.

Paul's life as a celibate is to be preferred. The Lord would return soon. The Christian must live for that imminent coming and not be tied to the relationships and attachments of this world. Don't worry about your status, whether free person or slave, for we are all one in Christ. Divorce must be avoided at all costs. Paul's rules reflecting both the words he heard that Jesus spoke as well as his own feelings had become the ethic of the church living within the expectation of Christ's immediate return. Later, the church would modify Paul's ethic as it was realized that the Christian must live for the long haul in the present order. Paul's words on divorce and on celibacy as the preferred way of life must not be taken any more literally by the church today than are his words about remaining slaves until the Lord comes. How often the church chooses which words of scripture to take literally and which to brush over. The church today proclaims the sacredness of life, of relationships and of marriage. That understanding is inherent in everything Paul wrote.

Notice that one Christian in the family brought salvation to the entire family. It is out of this understanding that infant baptism bacame a practice in the church.

The Gospel readings:

A surprising statement is read on Tuesday:". . . but whoever blasphemes against the Holy Spirit never has forgiveness, but is guilty of eternal sin" (Mark 3:29). Though we cannot know exactly what Jesus had in mind when he made this statement, it is evident that one cannot be healed and forgiven by the Spirit if one denies the power of the Spirit.

Earlier in the gospel readings we heard of the calling of Jesus' disciples and his healing ministry. This week we turn to a section in which the disciples are instructed for their mission in the world through the use of parables. They receive their first test of will and faith while in a boat on the tossing lake.

The scene opens with Jesus teaching a crowd of people by the lakeside. He must step into a boat in order to move far enough out from the people to be seen and heard by them.

His voice would carry naturally over the waters. Jesus proceeds to tell three parables, all with a similar point: the parable of the sower, the parable of the seed growing by itself, and the parable of the mustard seed. God is bringing in the kingdom. (The presence and power of Jesus is proof enough of that.) Though we may now barely discern the kingdom, it will come in its own good time, and its fulfillment will be beyond our wildest expectations. In other words, Jesus might have said, "Have faith my disciples. The seed of the kingdom is sown even now as I talk to you. The harvest will come in God's good time. Proclaim that harvest to all who will hear." But the writer of the gospel has taken the first of those parables and turned it into an allegory that explains why the gospel is not spreading faster that it is. Some seed is growing on rock and some among weeds, but those who do hear and receive the word, "bear fruit, thirtyfold, sixtyfold, or a hundredfold" (Mark 4:20). So, don't worry about the wasted seed among the many who seem not to be receiving the gospel. Rejoice, instead, at the harvest produced by the few.

Part of Mark's concern in writing the gospel was to deal with the question that bothered the church of his time: "Why were not more people convinced that Jesus was the Messiah when his miracles and powerful acts of new life should have been so obvious to everyone? Part of the explanation, Mark believed, lay in the hidden nature of Jesus' words and acts (Mark 4:9-12). It was God's will that the Word would remain a treasure for the few and a mystery to the many. That is why Jesus taught secretly and spoke in strange parables, Mark explains. The other gospel writers did not share this view.

Friday's reading describes the calming of the seas. This brief account is very symbolic. The roaring and heaving seas are calmed and separated by God at creation, we remember from the first chapter of the Book of Genesis. The power of God to separate the land from the sea was a sign of his creative power in the face of chaos. Psalm 74:12-14 describes that great act of creation poetically. Psalm 65:7 speaks of the power of God to act upon the storm at sea and to bring calm to creation and humanity. Jesus is the embodiment of God's power. He comes to bring calm out of chaos and fear, and a new creation happens is his presence. Followers of Jesus may expect struggle and "tossing seas" in their lives, but they must trust in the creating God even in the face of chaos.

The strange story of the Gerasene demoniac is shared on Saturday. This story needs to be read with the poet's eye as well as with the historian's interest. Jesus comes to drive chaos and disorder from the man's life, just as he had stilled the chaos of the water. He can do with the demons what he wills. He has that kind of power over chaos, evil and darkness. He can bring sanity out of madness. The death of the pigs may be shocking to the modern reader, but the story would have provided humor to a people who considered swine unclean.

The third week of Lent

The Old Testament readings:

Joseph's golden goblet is carefully placed in Benjamin's baggage along with the silver that the brothers had brought to pay for the grain. Soon after leaving the city, Joseph's steward apprehends them with the accusation that one of them has taken the master's cup. Joseph will now see how faithful his half brothers are toward his brother, Benjamin. Their response to Joseph's test will determine whether there is reconciliation within the family. The brothers could easily leave Benjamin behind and flee the country. On Monday, we read that Judah takes a stand for the honor of the brothers. They will not return home without Benjamin, he explains to Joseph. Judah takes Benjamin's place and becomes Joseph's slave.

The scene described in Tuesday's reading is one of the reconciliation between Joseph and his brothers. Joseph quickly reveals God's plan for the salvation of Israel that has now become clear to him. The painful trials that Joseph has undergone were God's plan for the saving of Israel. ". . . for God sent me before you to preserve life. . . And God sent me before you to preserve for a remnant on earth, and to keep alive for you many survivors. . . So it was not you who sent me here, but God. . ." (Gen 45:5,7,8) (*Genesis, a Bible Commentary for Teaching and Preaching,* Walter Brueggemann, John Knox Press, page 345). What had begun as an evil act had been turned to the salvation of the people. Joseph led the way for his family, Israel. Jesus' words to his disciples come to my mind as I read this passage. "In my Father's house are many rooms; if it were not so, would I have told you that I go to prepare a place for you? And when I go and prepare a place for you, I will come again and take you to myself, that here I am you may be also" (John 14:2-3).

Wednesday's and Thursday's texts provide us with glimpses of the joyful reunion between Joseph and his father and the settling of the whole family in Egypt. Pharaoh is more than generous to his favored minister, allowing the family to settle in the finest section of the land if they wish.

Joseph's great skill as an administrator occupies our attention of Friday, but his skill is mixed with an ominous foreshadowing of Israel's own oppression in Egypt that came to later generations. The freedom of the Egyptians is compromised as Joseph buys up all the lands of the peoples in exchange for seed and food. Private lands become Pharaoh's lands, with the people paying a fifth of their crop to Pharaoh for the right to farm the land that once had been theirs.

The Epistle readings:

With thoughts of Christ's imminent return in mind, Paul urges the Corinthians to remain celibate. One who was married would be distracted from serving Christ. The Christian must be ready to travel light during the short period before Jesus' return and let go of relationships and concerns that distract one from the coming reign of Christ. Paul's words still guide some Christians: The Roman Catholic insistance on celibate priests, for example, and celibate living in religious orders of several Christian communions.

The superior attitude of some of the Christians in the Corinthian church are Paul's next concern in his letter. Recent converts to Christ and some of the brothers and sisters who still feel bound by dietary restrictions of the Torah, refrain from eating meat purchased in the market place because it may have been sacrificed to a pagan god. Their argument is that to eat such meat is to be joined to the worship of the pagan god. The Christian could be contaminated without knowing it. Other Christians in Corinth flaunt their new-found freedom in Christ by openly eating the meat without regard to how their actions affect their brothers and sisters in the faith. Paul's words to the church are clear. Though the eating of meat could not destroy one's relationship to Christ, if the conscience of another Christian is offended by the practice, then the meat must not be eaten in their presence. The duty of love must outweigh the freedom enjoyed in the gospel.

Having admonished the Corinthians to curb their freedom so as not to cause offense to the weaker brethren, Paul reminds them that he has practiced such restraint himself in his life with them. He had freedom to be married and freedom to expect support from them in return for bringing them the gospel. But Paul would not compromise his witness by putting himself in a position where others might claim that he profited from the gospel. To the Jew, he became like a Jew even though he lived with the knowledge that the ritual code of the Torah was superseded by the freedom of the gospel. To the gentiles he spoke like a gentile in order to win them to the gospel. He lived and breathed as one training for an athletic event. Nothing less would do. No distractions could deter him. His life of total dedication was to be an example for the Corinthians.

Paul speaks to the Corinthians with an authority earned from his seeing the risen Christ on the road to Damascus (1 Cor 9:1). Thus, he can speak in the name of Christ and he can speak out of his own personal feelings as an apostle. He carefully makes a distinction between the two sources as he states his interim ethic to the church.

For the Christians who felt they had already won their salvation through baptism and through participating in the Lord's Supper, Paul has a severe warning. The Israelites had their "baptism" as they went through the Sea of Reeds (Red Sea) and as they walked within the cloud that guided them by day. They had the water and the bread offered them by God in the wilderness. (Paul refers to the manna of the wilderness and to the water that came from the rock that Moses struck at Horeb and in the wilderness of Zin.) The Israelites, in other words, were fed by the Lord at the Eucharist, but that did not save them when they succumbed to the temptations encountered on their pilgrimage. As a result, they died never having seen the Promised land of the Lord. The wilderness becomes a metaphor in Paul's mind. The Corinthians are to take warning and resist the temptations encountered on their pilgrimage. However, the Lord would not test them beyond what they could bear. Though Paul does not mention Jesus' temptation in the wilderness, that image comes to mind as living imagery for the Christian. After baptism the testing begins in earnest.

The Gospel readings:

After words and acts of instruction, Jesus sends his disciples out to proclaim the coming kingdom. They have witnessed the power in their own lives. They have been instructed, through parable and vivid experience, in the meaning of that coming kingdom. Now it is their turn to act in Jesus' name, we learn in Tuesday's reading.

The death of John the Baptist colors our midweek reading with a grim and foreboding feeling. John dies for standing for the Word and truth of God in the face of evil. His ministry is rejected by the authority, and he dies an unjust death. John's death points ahead to Jesus' death.

The familiar story of the feeding of the 5,000 is the appointed lesson for Thursday. One of the beautiful images of the kingdom, or reign, of God prevalent in Jesus' time was the "messianic banquet." At the dawn of the new age, ". . . many will come from east and west and sit at table with Abraham, Isaac, and Jacob in the kingdom of heaven. . ." (Matt 8:11). The Lord will be the host at the banquet, and all peoples will feed and drink at the Lord's table. This feeding incident on the hillside can be seen as a foretaste of that banquet, just as the Eucharist is a foretaste of our life to come at the Lord's table in the kingdom. Notice the Eucharist-like words and actions in the description of Jesus taking the bread, breaking and blessing it, and then distributing it to the assembled people. Jesus comes to gather the family of God. Like the father of the Jewish home or the religious leader of a group of Jewish men, he blesses, breaks and distributes the bread in table fellowship as an expression of the people's relationship to the living God.

Feeding stories were not unique to Jesus. See 2 Kings 4:42-44 for a similar story told about the great prophet, Elisha. He, also, was remembered as having fed a group of people miraculously. As people in Jesus' time heard the story, they would have connected Jesus with the great prophets of the Old Testament.

As you read Friday's lesson, your mind may move back to last Friday when we read that Jesus quieted the storm and then came to shore to offer healing. This calming/healing motif is followed in today's reading, only this time the miracle of calming is heightened. Jesus is seen walking on the water. He is about to pass the disciples by when he notices their fear. Again, Jesus exercises power over the elements by calming the storm. He walks over the waters that represented death and chaos to ancient peoples. Some scholars feel that this event may have actually been a resurrection appearance, but the power of the story in the early church lay in the hope that the event held out to a church living in confusion, persecution and fear.

Think about St. Paul's controversy with the Jewish authorities as you read Saturday's lesson. Paul's insistence that gentiles could enter into relationship with Christ without following the strict dietary rituals of the orthodox Jew is given the authority of Jesus in these passages. It is not what goes into us that stands between us and holiness. It is what comes out of our lives that makes us holy in the sight of God. We dare not substitute empty ritual for life-giving service to the Lord in our lives. Realize the radical nature of these words as you read them. The ancient practices followed by generations of faithful Jews is questioned. Can we understand the reaction of the Jewish authorities in the face of Jesus' words and actions? How do we respond in church and nation to those who question the very heart of our actions and assumptions about life?

The fourth week of Lent

The Old Testament readings:

As we begin our reading of the Joseph saga this fourth week of Lent, we learn the great promise of God's covenant with Israel is passed from one generation to the next. Old Jacob, lying on his death bed, manages to muster his strength for the blessing of his grandsons, Ephraim and Manasseh. These two sons were the patriarchs of two of the twelve tribes of Israel. Ephraim is by far the stronger tribe in history. (The name of Ephraim was often applied to the whole northern kingdom of Israel.) Thus, the recorder of the beautiful scene of blessing took pains to point out that Jacob knows of the prominence that Ephraim is to play in history. Jacob deliberately chooses to give Joseph's younger son, Ephraim, the primary blessing usually reserved for the older son.

Monday's reading is a series of what appear to be predictions of what will happen to the tribes that come forth from each of the sons of Jacob. In fact, the sayings are more likely a collection of tribal aphorisms that developed after the twelve tribes of Israel settled in Canaan.

Jacob asks to be buried back in Canaan, and when Joseph later dies, his last request is that his bones be returned to the land promised to Abraham, Isaac and Jacob. The identity of Israel as God's covenant people must never be forgotten. That is why burial in the Promised Land was so essential.

Our reading of the Book of Genesis, begun the first week after Epiphany, ends on Wednesday as we move into the Book of Exodus for the continuing saga of Israel's life in Egypt. "Now there arose a new king over Egypt, who did not know Joseph." Now the descendants of Joseph are seen only as a threat to Egypt's security and as a source of slave labor for the building of store cities. The familiar pattern of Israel's story is again heard in Thursday's reading. The more Israel's enemies work to destroy the people, the stronger they become.

Friday's reading includes a familiar Sunday school story. The baby Moses is placed in a water-tight basket and hidden among the reeds by the Nile. Pharaoh's daughter finds the infant and decides to raise the child herself. Though raised in Pharaoh's court, Moses carries the memory and the promise of his people with him. When he observes the oppression of his own people as a young man, he responds by killing an Egyptian. This precipitant action leads to Moses' flight to the land of Midian, a territory lying along the eastern shore of the Gulf of Aqaba in what is now Saudi Arabia, just south of Jordan. The Midianites were a nomadic people, however, so that the "land of Midian" mentioned in Exodus 2:15 may have included the Sinai wilderness near Mt. Sinai. In any case, Moses becomes a simple sheepherder, tending his father-in-law's flocks. That is, he is a sheepherder until the day he sees the vision of a burning bush. Out of that burning bush comes a voice that identifies itself to Moses by the strange name of "I Am Who I Am" (Exodus 3:14).

This name is the source of the name "Yahweh" (in the King James Version, "Jehovah"). "There are various understandings of this unusual name. One way of interpreting it is to realize that the God who identified himself to Moses, was the "God of what is happening." In other words, "I am who I am" is "I am what is happening to you" or "I am your story or history." (*Sharing Our Biblical Story*, Joseph Russell, page 47, Winston Press.)

The Epistle readings:

This is a heavyweight week in the Epistle to the Corinthians, for we deal not only with Paul's feelings about the Eucharist, but with his well-known words about spiritual gifts.

Paul has just assured the Corinthians that they did not need to worry about eating meat that might have been sacrificed to pagan gods. As we begin our reading this week, Paul is concerned about Christians who knowingly take part in pagan rituals that include eating sacrificial meat. They should know that as they take the cup and share in the loaf of the Eucharist they are "sharing in the body of Christ" (1 Cor 10:16). Consequently, they also realize that knowingly to eat meat sacrificed to a demon is to reject their oneness in Christ and to join themselves to the demon! In this negative admonition about refraining from pagan sacrificial meals, we also have a positive statement about the Eucharist. To share the cup and bread of Christ is actually to share in the body of Christ. It is to become one with Christ and one with the whole people of Christ, the church. Paul then returns to his earlier concern about accidentally eating meat sacrificed to idols. Eat the meat sold in the market place, Paul says. After all, ". . .the earth is the Lord's and everything in it" (1 Cor 10:26). Our freedom in Christ must always be tempered by our concerns for the whole community. This is the model that Paul offered in his life at Corinth. This must be the way of life for Christians living out the gospel in their lives in every age.

On Tuesday we move into the third section of the letter dealing with communal worship. We get some fascinating insight into the life of the Corinthian church and probably of other churches established by Paul as well. The Eucharist was obviously celebrated as a part of a meal. Our church potluck suppers may be closer to the Eucharist as celebrated in Corinth than the formal liturgies we celebrate today. The problem was the fellowship meals had begun to degenerate into factional free-for-alls in which the better-off Christians did not share with the poorer members of the church. The cup of Eucharist was lost in the drinking of many cups of wine. What a shocking scene for Paul to contemplate. He reminds the Corinthians of the sacred nature of their Eucharistic meal by recalling the words Jesus used on the night he was handed over to die. These words, of course, form the heart of our Eucharistic act. Since the gospels were written after Paul's epistles, the words we read this week are our earliest written witness to the Eucharist and to the words Jesus used as he shared cup and bread.

If the bread and cup are taken in a way that the living presence of Christ is not recognized and lived out in the life of the community, then the people take the sacrament to their condemnation. No wonder the church has traditionally preceded the act of Eucharist with confession. The passing of the Peace at the Eucharist is another vivid reminder to the Christian today that we must live in community with brother and sister before partaking of the Body and Blood of Christ. As Paul's words were taken more and more literally over the years, the dreadful nature of the sacrament overshadowed the gift of God's presence revealed in it. We can see why the Eucharist was received so rarely by Christians in later generations.

"Jesus is Lord" may be the earliest Christian creed. It is a statement of absolute faith in Jesus as the Lord of all. The Apostles' Creed and the Nicene Creed are elaborations of that simple statement of faith. "We believe in one Lord, Jesus Christ, the only Son of God." Paul tells the Corinthians that to repeat the creed in faith is to evidence the Spirit in one's life. That is the point Paul makes as he launches into his beautiful words about the unity of life in the Spirit. Paul opened his letter to the Corinthians with his concern about factions in the church. He has written about false pride and the need to live for the good of the whole community of the church. Now he reminds the Corinthians about the unity of the Spirit they share that makes them all equal in the body of Christ. Each one has different gifts but they are all gifts of the Spirit. The church must live with an understanding that each gift, though different, is essential. If one part of the body suffers or is rejected, the whole body suffers.

We conclude our week of reading with a delineation of ministries that were recognized in Paul's churches. Apostles come first, then prophets and so on in descending order. Not everyone is an apostle, or prophet, teacher or healer. Not everyone speaks in estatic tongues or interprets them. Paul's descending order of ministry would seem to deny the equality of gifts he has just spoken of, but his point is that no one should take pride in what his gift is. They should always aspire for "the higher gifts." That statement leads Paul into the beautiful words from the 13th chapter of First Corinthians that are so often quoted. "If I speak in the tongues of men and angels, but have not love, I am a noisy gong or a clanging cymbal" (1Cor 13:1). Often read out of context, this passage really crowns all that we have been reading this week. We cannot take pride in the gifts that God has given us for ministry. That false pride was the downfall of the Corinthians and the downfall of each one of us. The moment a gift of the Spirit becomes a badge of distinction and a means of judging another person, then the Christian must stand under the judgement of the greater demand of love.

The Gospel readings:

Notice the exhaustion of Jesus as you begin this week's reading. Jesus would remove himself from the demands of the people if only for a moment, but rest is impossible. A gentile woman places a demand on him for healing. Jesus' blunt words to her may shock us as we read them today: "Let the children first be fed, for it is not right to take the children's bread and throw it to the dogs" (Mark 7:27). The tone of Jesus' voice and the expression on his face are not seen nor heard by us, but in any case, the woman throws his words back to him. Perhaps amused at her quickness, he responds to her request. Ironically, it is a woman considered by some "unfit to receive the children's bread" who shows the faith in Jesus that "the children" themselves lack. Perhaps it is the irony of this acceptance-in-contrast-to-rejection that causes Jesus to speak to the woman, using a common expression of disdain applied to gentiles.

One healing is quickly followed by another, as the deaf and mute man comes to him. In contrast to the "dumb" people unable and unwilling to proclaim the new age that has dawned with Jesus, this "dumb" man now speaks. Isaiah's words come true: "On that day the deaf shall hear the words of a book, and out of their gloom and darkness the eyes of the blind shall see" (29:18).

You are not seeing double as you study Saturday's lesson. Last week we read that Jesus fed 5,000 people, and now we read that Jesus fed 4,000 people, in a very similar account. Many scholars feel that this is simply a "doublet," or repeating of the one story.

The Pharisees demand a sign from Jesus who has denied that God would send signs "in this generation." The disciples, however, have been seeing signs all around them as they followed Jesus, especially in the miracle of the loaves! Despite the signs, they remain blind to the significance of Jesus' life among them. We then read of the healing of the blind man at Bethsaida. The blind man can now see far more clearly than those blind disciples! Real sight begins to come to Peter, however, as he realizes who Jesus is, but he still cannot see as God would have him see. He cannot see that to be Messiah Jesus must suffer and die.

This passage marks the hinge point of the Gospel of Mark. From this point on in our daily reading of Mark, our faces will be set toward Jerusalem as Jesus moves to his inevitable destiny.

The collect for Fridays, on page 99 of The Book of Common Prayer, sets the theme for Thursday's reading:

Almighty God, whose most dear Son went not up to joy but first he suffered pain, and entered not into glory before he was crucified: Mercifully grant that we, walking in the way of the cross, may find it none other than the way of life and of peace.

The disciples of Jesus must bear the cross in every age. These words stand in stark contrast to the assumption that when one follows Jesus, life will be easy and profitable.

On Friday you may want to refer to Exodus 24:1-18 for background to appreciate the significance of the transfiguration. Moses went "up into the mountain" for a revelation of the Law. Jesus brings a law not written on stone, but written on the hearts of the people (see Jeremiah 31:31). Several other points need to be kept in mind: Elijah was the great prophet of Israel who lived in the time of King Ahab and Queen Jezebel (1 Kings). Tradition held that it would be Elijah who would return at the coming of the Messiah to herald the day of the Lord. The Feast of Booths was a joyous fall harvest festival in which shelters were erected from harvest stalks and vines to celebrate

God's presence with the people as they wandered in the wilderness. According to Zechariah 14:16-19, all nations would celebrate the feast together at the coming of the final day of the Lord. Peter's mention of the tent, or booth, or tabernacle, is a reference to that great expectation. Tradition held that Elijah's role at the ushering in of the day of the Lord was to purify the people of God, to turn them back to Torah. Jesus saw this as the role of John the Baptist, who had already come and been killed by Herod. Jesus was not to be confused with Elijah. He was to be the Suffering Servant of the Lord, the servant who would die so that healing and salvation would come for all people. When Moses came down from the mountain after receiving the tablets of the law, he was immediately met with confusion and loss of faith on the part of the people (Exodus 32). In his absence, they had created a golden calf to worship. Now as Jesus comes down from the "Mountain of Revelation," he also meets with the loss of faith and confusion among his disciples. No wonder his anguished words: "How long must I put up with this people?'

The fifth week of Lent

The Old Testament readings:

God's promise of deliverance to the Israelites is met by Moses' doubt. How can this be? is the question on Moses' lips. Three strange miracles are produced by the God who speaks from the bush. Moses finds that he can turn his staff into a snake and then grab the snake by the tail and turn it back into a staff. His hand turns leprous when placed in the folds of his cloak and is immediately cured when he places his hand back into the folds of his cloak. Water turns to blood as it is poured onto the ground.

The magic elment of God's action appears again during the week as Moses actually competes with the magicians of Egypt for Pharaoh's attention. As you read from the Book of Exodus this week, remember that these stories were told orally from generation to generation. Certain details of the story show the art of the story teller rather than the accuracy of the more literal minded reporter. The heightening of the account becomes a running theological commentary as the story unfolds. What happened in Egypt and in the Sinai wilderness, the story tellers make clear, was no mere accident of nature. God was at work liberating the Israelites from Egyptian oppression and guiding them toward a new destiny in covenant and in the Promised Land.

At first the Israelites receive Moses' news of God's deliverance with appreciation, but when Pharaoh's overseers are instructed to force the Israelites to work harder as a result of Moses' and Aaron's visit to the ruler, the people's praise turns to angry complaint. On Tuesday, we encounter the first of many complaints Moses will make before the Lord. In the coming weeks, we'll be hearing that anguished cry raised to the Lord time and again as the Israelites lose heart in the long trek toward the Promised Land.

The first of the 10 plagues are encountered in Wednesday's ṛection. The waters of the Nile are turned into blood right before Pharaoh's eyes. Note that the magicians of Egypt are able to accomplish the same act of magic so that Pharaoh remains unmoved. For the balance of the week, we move through the other plagues that strike Egypt but mysteriously do not disturb the life of the Israelites. At week's end, we hear the announcement of the death of the first-born animals and humans that will come one dark and fear-filled night in the coming days. The death of the first-born leads to Israel's release from slavery by a desperate Pharaoh, but that account will not be read until the first week of Easter.

All of the plagues that struck Egypt in the time of Moses are still present realities in today's world. Pestilence, hail storms, disease and polluted waters are ever present dangers. The plagues that struck Egypt probably happened over a period of several years, but in each case, Israel saw those signs not as natural phenomena but as direct actions of God that struck fear into the heart of Pharaoh and courage into the minds of the Israelites. As the story was related over many generations, it took its present form that reads like a litany, praising God's power in the face of those who act to oppress the people. We are not reading history in this account as much as we are reading a theological statement about God's call to Israel and the liberation of the people from oppression. These natural events become signs of faith for the Jew and later for the Christian. We make the same kind of faith-statement when we connect healing with a sign of God's power experienced in our lives. Some may see healing as good fortune or simply the skill of the attending physician. The Christian sees healing as a gift of God who works through the hands of the physician as well as through the faith of a person.

The Epistle readings:

Paul opened his letter to the Corinthians expressing his concern about the divisions existing within the church. Not only were the people divided as to whom they considered their leaders, but they must also have been divided as to the question of who had the greater gifts of the Spirit. It would seem that those who spoke in ecstatic speech (glossolalia) were causing the greater problem for the young church. If Christians spoke "with the tongues of angels" but did not have love, they were simply ". . .a noisy gong or a clanging cymbal" (1 Cor 13:1). The Christian's first concern must be for the building up of the church. If love is the first test of whether one is truly sharing the gifts of the Spirit, the building up of the body of Christ is the second test. Words that don't inspire or instruct the faithful are destructive, Paul warned. In First Corinthians 14:21, Paul quotes the prophet Isaiah as proof that speaking in strange tongues without interpretation is reserved for "unbelievers" or pagans and not for the church. (Actually, Paul was taking Isaiah's words out of context. Isaiah was warning the people of Judah that if they did not listen to God's prophets, they would have to listen to the strange speech of the Assyrians who would invade their land as a sign of God's displeasure.) Paul then goes on to lay down restrictions for those who would speak in tongues.

On Wednesday we leave Paul's First Epistle to the Corinthians and move into the second chapter of Paul's Second Epistle to the Corinthians. Since the 15th chapter of First Corinthians deals directly with the resurrection, we will wait until Easter week to read it.

As Lent draws to a close and we focus more on the passion of our Lord, Paul's own suffering for the gospel and for the unity of the church makes an appropriate parallel to the suffering of Jesus that is remembered so vividly next week during Holy Week. The sudden shift from First to Second Corinthians simply enables us to stay with Paul as he expresses his own understanding of what it means to be an apostle for Christ. Suffering is an integral part of that ministry, Paul discovered. As we enter our own Holy Week experience this year and every year, we are called to a life that demands that we share the weight of the cross ourselves. We are the continuing sacrifice of Christ on the cross of today's world. As Paul describes his understanding of ministry, may we identify our own ministry with his. "For while we live we are always being given up to death for Jesus' sake, so that the life of Jesus may be manifested in our mortal flesh. So death is at work in us, but life in you" (2 Cor 4:11-12). The bearing of the cross also reveals the new life of Christ that springs up out of the struggle that comes from living for Christ. As we live in union with Christ and reflect his glory, we are transfigured into the likeness of Christ as the relationship deepens.

The Gospel readings:
To appreciate fully this week's readings from the Gospel of Mark, picture the church to whom this gospel is addressed. It is a church under persecution. The converts have been promised eternal life in the risen Christ, but they are now experiencing martyrdom, ridicule, rejection and suffering. It is in this painful situation that the Gospel of Mark was written. This section of Mark, starting with Mark 8:34 and continuing through the end of chapter 10, is a teaching section for new converts and for the church in general. "This is what it means to be a follower of the risen Christ," Mark is saying; "This is what you can expect out of your discipleship."

Tuesday's reading speaks strong words for the church. The "little ones," or recent converts, must not be tempted to forego the gospel for the sake of present comfort. To tempt the weak is to invite instant condemnation for yourself. Temptation to sin must be resisted at all costs. The hand would reach out to sin, the foot would be the part of the body that would direct one to leave the gospel, the eye would see the opportunity for sin. "Cut them out," if need be, to avoid the sin. The closing words for Monday warn the Christian that being tested by "salt and fire" is part of what life-in-Christ means. The Christian is to "salt," or flavor the environment. Tasteless salt is worthless.

Marriage and divorce within the Christian covenant is the focus of Wednesday's readings. Jesus' words seem restrictive in our age when divorce is recognized by the church. Remember that in Jesus' day, wives could be easily divorced by their husbands; wives had very few rights of their own. Jesus' teaching on divorce protects the woman and affirms her status in her husband's house. Historically, the church has exercised the privilege of modifying Jesus' teaching in the light of the guidance of the Holy Spirit. Matthew 18:18 has been seen as the authority for this interpretive aspect of the church's life: "Truly, I say to you, whatever you bind on earth shall be bound in heaven, and whatever you loose on earth shall be loosed in heaven."

Discipleship also results in a reversal of expectations, we learn on Friday. James and John expect reward and prestige. Instead, they will receive the cup and baptism of martyrdom. One who is a disciple is one who serves, rather than one who is served. Think of the impact of those words on a church suffering from persecution today. These are the people who truly know the sense and urgency of the reign of God. Jesus' words about affluence come home to us.

Holy Week

The Old Testament readings:

During Holy Week we step out of our sequential reading of the Book of Exodus in order to read from the Book of Lamentations. This book was written during the deportations and the destruction of Jerusalem by the Babylonian armies that went on from 597 to 587 B.C. Lamentations gives us a firsthand account of the feelings associated with the tragic experience that came to the once proud city of Jerusalem. We read in poetic form the scene described for us by one who witnessed the horrors of that moment in our people's history. The book picks up the mood and feeling of Holy Week so well that is has been assigned for reading at this time in the church since early times. The lament over the fall of Jerusalem at the hands of the hated enemy reflects the lament over the death of Jesus. All hope was lost in 587. All hope was lost as Jesus was led to Calvary. Evil seemed the victor over the love and power of God. Allow the feelings of Lamentations to inform your prayers and thoughts during the coming week. As we touch our own feelings of despair we can sense anew the cry of hope raised on Easter Day.

The great theme of the exodus and the wilderness wandering of our biblical ancestors formed a metaphor in the mind of the primitive church, a metaphor that shapes our celebration of Lent and Easter to this day. Our baptism is our experience of passing through the waters of the Sea of Reeds (or Red Sea). We wander in our Sinai wilderness feeling tested and tried in this life but always led on by the covenant that points to the promise of the reign of God. The season of Lent symbolizes that life pilgrimage. As this great season of Lent draws to a close, we've trod the path of our biblical ancestors in their wilderness trek. We've faced the awful vacuum of life without hope expressed in Lamentations and in the traditions of Holy Week. We can now prepare to celebrate the victory of Christ that gives us a foretaste of the reign of God. Out of lament comes the cry of new life. Out of the wilderness wandering comes an awareness that God has been walking with us all this time. We see again the power of the lectionary as it guides us day after day in our life's journey.

In the early centuries of the church, converts to the faith were baptized on Easter Day, a tradition encouraged in The Book of Common Prayer today. At baptism we enter into Christ's death so that we can be raised to new life with him in the resurrection.

The Epistle readings:

The epistle readings also reflect the mood of the season of Lent and of Holy Week. We read part of Second Corinthians chapters 2 through 4 last week. This week, we go back to the beginning of the epistle where Paul talks about suffering with Christ in order to share in the strength and comfort of Christ. "For as we share abundantly in Christ's sufferings, so through Christ we share abundantly in comfort too" (1 Cor 1:5). To be in the service of Christ means to share in the suffering of Christ. That is the Christian's calling. Paul suffered in his relationship with the Corinthians. The struggle that he encountered as he dealt with a church so split by factions and by moral problems led him into a deeper sense of Christ's comfort and presence. The terrible strife that he encountered in the province of Asia, led Paul to a deeper awareness of the power of God's own pain, our own fear and sense of death. The traditions of Holy Week lead us to Golgotha and the cross, to the sepulcher in the garden. The readings assigned for Holy Week go hand in hand with the traditions of the church so that we may find within ourselves and within the struggle of church, nation and society, those aspects of our own lives that are being redeemed by Christ.

The portion of Second Corinthians we read during these two weeks was written after Paul received word from Corinth that the church had acted on Paul's earlier letter. Unity had been restored. The guilty person had been confronted and had accepted the discipline of the church. Now it was time to offer forgiveness and seek reconciliation, Paul wrote them. This theme, too, is a part of the Holy Week message. Easter is the assurance of Christ's forgiveness in the present time and in the age to come. Paul wrote with this assurance. He wrote from the sense of intense relief and joy at a relationship restored with the church at Corinth.

On Maundy Thursday we read a portion of First Corinthians which was read just two weeks ago during the fourth week of Lent. This deals with the sacred nature of the Eucharist, appropriate words to hear on this day that we remember the Last Supper.

The Good Friday lection is from First Peter. Some scholars feel that this letter was composed of portions of an early baptismal liturgy. We may be reading words offered to converts just prior to their Easter baptism. "You know that you were ransomed from the futile ways inherited from your fathers. . .with the precious blood of Christ. . ." (1 Peter 1:18-19). On this day that we remember that "precious blood of Christ," we must also remember the awe-filled convenant framed upon that cross that marks our lives.

Holy Saturday marks the day of Jesus' burial, his time of "rest" between death on Good Friday and his rising again on Easter morning. Saturday is also the Sabbath of the Jewish calendar, a time when all the faithful of God are to rest as God rested on the "seventh day" of creation. This "rest" on the Sabbath became a metaphor in the early church for the final rest with God when the reign of God had come fully. The Sabbath is a foretaste of the messianic age, in other words, or a foretaste of heaven. That is why the sense of the Sabbath is still important for the Christian to follow. Note the collect for Saturdays, page 99, The Book of Common Prayer:

> Almighty God, who after the creation of the world rested from all your works and sanctified a day of rest for all your creatures: Grant that we, putting away all earthly anxieties, may be duly prepared for the service of your sanctuary, and that our rest here upon earth may be a preparation for the eternal rest promised to your people in heaven...

This background may make the epistle assigned for Holy Saturday a little easier to understand. The writer of Hebrews uses the story of our biblical ancestors in the wilderness as a warning. They failed to enter God's rest (the Promised Land) because of their lack of faith. Christians have another chance at finding that rest. A new promise awaits them, but it is a promise that can only be realized as they follow in faith where Joshua/Jesus leads them. (Joshua and Jesus are actually the same name, Jesus being a Greek derivative of the Hebrew Joshua.) The lection for this day calls us to enter into the rest of God as expressed in the Sabbath tradition and more especially into the rest of Jesus' burial. Jesus, our great high priest, opens up to us access to the very throne of God. He entered into our human weakness, even our death, to point the way to that throne. His human weakness is marked by burial in a grave, his rest between death and resurrection.

The Gospel readings:

On Monday we read the events thought to have happened on the Monday of what we today call Holy Week. It is now the day after the triumphal entry, and Jesus again enters the city after spending the night at Bethany, a town about 1 3/4 miles from Jerusalem. The curse of the fig tree can best be understood as a parable told by Jesus (see Luke 13:6-9) that the writer of Mark placed in the narrative to emphasize the point of what was happening in these final days. It serves as a commentary on the action we are witnessing through the Word.

A little background is necessary to appreciate the cleansing of the Temple scene. Jesus was not upset with the money-changing and selling going on in the Temple. That was essential for the carrying on of the rites of Jerusalem. It was the unfair practices that had grown up around the money-changing and sale of sacrificial animals that aroused his anger. But of more importance, Jesus was acting out a prophetic drama to make a clear statement to the people that he was announcing the inauguration of the messianic age. Take a moment now and read Jeremiah 7:1-16, Isaiah 56:7, and Malachi 3:3-5 so that you can see Jesus' activity here through the same perspective as the people of his time. You may also want to read Jeremiah 13:1-11 and Isaiah 20:1-6 for examples of similar dramatic actions by the prophets.

Jesus' actions at the Temple were not lost on the authorities. They moved quickly to entrap him in order to discredit him among the people and to find grounds on which he could be brought before the Jewish and Roman courts.

The gospel readings reflect the feelings of Holy Week. We've been reading the Gospel of Mark all during Lent. As Holy Week comes, we find our sequential reading leads us naturally into Jesus' approach to Jerusalem and his passion. The readings for Maundy Thursday, Good Friday and Holy Saturday were chosen to express the theme for each of those major days— Eucharist, death and burial.

The first week of Easter

The church's celebration of Easter begins with the first Eucharist of Easter Day and continues through the feast of Pentecost 50 days later. During this season we concentrate on the significance and joy of the resurrection. Just as one seventh of each week is focused on the resurrection with the celebration of Sunday, so one seventh of the year is focused on the great central tenet of the Christian faith.

Those who were baptized on Easter Day in the primitive church were brought into the body of Christ during the Great Fifty Days. Where Lent helped to prepare the catechumens for their entrance into the church, the Great Fifty Days was a time of helping the recently baptized examine the meaning of their new life in the body of Christ. This was, therefore, a great period of celebration as well as a significant time for teaching about and living out the meaning of Christian life. We have much to learn from our biblical ancestors as we seek to gather new people into our congregations. The ancient task of training new Christians continues to be the focus of the lectionary readings during the Easter season. Each year the church rehearses the teaching and practice of the faith for old and new Christians alike.

The Old Testament readings:
This week we pick up the sequential reading of the Book of Exodus that was interrupted for Holy Week. Instructions for the strict following of the Jewish festival of Passover as it was practiced in later years were placed on the lips of Moses to provide a firm authority for the keeping of the feast. Every generation of Israel would be called to remember the mighty acts of God carried out on Israel's behalf. As they remembered the Lord's mighty acts in history, the people would perceive more readily the acts of God happening in every generation. To remember as a Jew or a Christian is not nostalgia for an earlier time; it is to bring the memory forward to the present moment. God is acting to save us, we realize, as we remember how God

was acting to save our people in an earlier time. The memory becomes a present reality, which is why remembering is such an essential act of faith.

The origin of the name, Passover, is explained in Monday's reading, along with an explanation for some of the Passover customs. Leaven was associated with corruption and evil among many people of the time. The explanation for prohibiting the use of leaven during Passover, however, was associated with the Exodus story. The people were in such a hurry to leave Egypt that they did not have time to add leaven to their dough. The ritual associated with the Passover conveyed the story as well as the words used to narrate the story.

The description of the death of Egypt's first born is a grim account. Israel read the events of history through the eye of theological understanding. When a plague descended upon the Egyptians and left the ghettos of the slaves untouched, God's blessing upon Israel and his curse upon the Egyptians was understood and remembered. The one night of death from disease may actually have been weeks of plague, but over time the facts were caught up into a creedal statement of belief that blended fact with faith statement. "God has acted dramatically for us," is the heart of the story.

A lamb was slaughtered and its blood smeared on the doorpost that awesome night. Israel remembered that act in their ritual, too. When the Passover was celebrated at the Temple in Jesus' day, pilgrims bought an unblemished lamb on the Temple grounds. Symbolically they laid their sins upon that lamb. The priests slaughtered it on the altar. The families then took their lamb, roasted it, and ate it for the Passover meal. As the lamb had died to save the people from disease at the time of the Exodus, so the lamb was slaughtered at the Temple to save the people from the results of their sins before God. The "lamb of God" was a sacrificial lamb. When Jesus died on the cross at Passover time, his death was quickly associated with the dying of the Passover lambs. Jesus was the perfect Passover lamb who died for the sins of all people in all times. At this season of Easter we see the origins of the primitive church's understanding of Jesus' death and our salvation in the light of his death.

The roots of Jesus' presentation in the Temple, as described in Luke 2:22-24, are found in Friday's reading. As a remembrance that the first born of Egypt died at the time of the Exodus, Israel must offer every first-born to God. This custom was common among the peoples who surrounded Israel, except that, in most cases, that first-born child was given to the gods as a human sacrifice. Not so for Israel. First-born sons were offered to God, but then were "redeemed" by the offering of an animal instead. The story in Genesis describing Abraham's sacrifice of his son, Isaac, was told as a precedent. Instead of Isaac, a ram was offered. So it was to be for every first-born male. According to Leviticus 12:1-8 a young ram was to be offered, whether the child was male or female. The poor who could not afford such an offering could offer two turtle doves or two young pigeons instead. From Luke's account of Jesus' presentation in the Temple, we realize that Mary and Joseph could only make the offering of the poor.

A pillar of cloud by day and a pillar of fire by night guided the people of the Exodus. As Christians gather for the Easter vigil, the paschal candle is carried in procession through the midst of the people as a remembrance of the pillar of fire. Christians remember that it is the light of Christ that leads us out of the bondage of darkness into the promise of the coming realm of God.

The Epistle readings:

This Easter week we look at Paul's beautiful words of faith based directly on the resurrection. In the 15th chapter of First Corinthians Paul gives us an outline of the gospel he has been preaching and teaching to the churches. The opening words read like Paul's own personal creed.

Paul defends his doctrine of the resurrection. Apparently some in the Corinthian church were questioning the fact and power of the resurrection. How could they be saying such a thing? "But if there is no resurrection of the dead, then Christ has not been raised; if Christ has not been raised, then our preaching is in vain and your faith is in vain" (1 Cor 15:13-14).

Wednesday's optional verse (1 Cor 15:29) is a strange statement about the practice of persons being baptized for those who have already died. Apparently this was a local practice in Corinth. Paul simply mentions it as another example of the faith people have in resurrection. "Since the mention is so unspecific and there is no information from any other New Testament writing, (nor, it may be added, in the apostolic fathers), the practice must be considered a curious anomaly, which apparently dropped out of view until revived by some second-and-third century sectarians." (1 Corinthians, by William F. Orr and James A. Walther, Anchor Bible, Doubleday and Co., p. 337.)

As you read from First Corinthians this week keep in mind that portions of this chapter are appointed for reading at the Burial of the Dead. These strong words of faith expressed by Paul have strengthened Christians in times of grief for generations.

On Saturday we turn to Paul's words of resurrection hope expressed in his Second Letter to the Corinthians: "Though our outer nature is wasting away, our inner nature is being renewed every day" (2 Cor 4:16). The body we have is really only temporary. God has something far more wonderful for us in store, a gift that Paul looks with growing anticipation to receiving.

The Gospel readings:

The gospel readings offer a selection of resurrection appearances. Saturday's reading, taken from Mark's gospel, contain Jesus' words to the Sadducees about the resurrection. The Sadducees refused to believe in the resurrection because it is not mentioned in the Torah. When God spoke to Moses in the wilderness, Jesus reminded them, he did not say to Moses that he *had been* the God of Abraham and Isaac. God identified himself as the God *who is* the God of Abraham and Isaac, a present reality. Further proof, right from the Torah, that life cannot be limited to the historic moment.

The second week of Easter

The Old Testament readings:

With the Lord's guidance and power, Moses was able to lead the Israelites out of Egypt, but the awesomeness of that night of flight was soon lost on the people as they complained to Moses "Is it because there are no graves in Egypt that you have taken us away to die in the wilderness?" (Ex 14:11). This is the kind of complaint Moses would hear for the next 40 years!

With the people facing the Red Sea and the dust of Pharaoh's chariots rising up on the horizon, the people had reason to cry out. The crossing of the Red Sea reads like a miracle of the first order. However, it is possible to read the story as the account of a natural event rather than a miracle. Read the following verses alone before looking at the entire account as it now stands in scripture: Exodus 14:5-7, 10-14, 19-20, second half of verse 21, and 24-25, second half of verse 27, and 30-31. Picture a large impassable marshland. During the night a warm wind blows. When the Israelites awaken in the morning, they are able to walk across that marsh on dry land. By the time Pharaoh's chariots arrive on the scene, the wind has died down and chariot wheels become clogged. Studies show that in the days of Moses what we now call the Red Sea was more likely a marsh area. Some translations use the name, Sea of Reeds, rather than Red Sea. As this story was told and retold and as the significance of the event was heightened, miraculous details of the deliverance were added. The complete narrative as it reads today appears to be strata of stories woven together over time. Scholars can now identify the layers through intricate linguistic study of the Hebrew.

When our biblical ancestors reached the other side of the marsh and saw Pharaoh's army turn back, Miriam picked up her tambourine and sang a song of triumph. Her original refrain is read on Tuesday in Exodus 15:21. This may well have been one of the earliest pieces of writing in the scriptures. Later writers expanded her refrain into the Song of Moses (Ex 15:1-18).

This is one of the canticles of Morning Prayer; here we see it in its context.

Now that the people were safe from Pharaoh's chariots, their thoughts turned to food and again they cried out. The bread, or manna, of the wilderness was God's response to this complaint. The daily manna, a sticky substance formed by insects and still found in the wilderness of Sinai, was to be shared equally. No one was to go hungry. The Sabbath bread, however, must be procured the day before, since no work could be done on the sacred day.

The crossing of the sea, the providing of bread, the plagues against the Egyptians can be seen as mighty miracles that defy explanation, or they can be seen as natural events that our people saw as signs of God's presence among them. This interpretation leaves us free today to look for signs of God's activity among us. Some may speak of luck or coincidence, but the biblical way of looking at life is set forth for us in the texts we read these Easter weeks. Reflect on life's experiences. See in those experiences the shepherding presence of God leading us from enslavement to a new promise. We, too, are on a journey, a journey made with fellow travelers in the wilderness of our time. God speaks to us in our thoughts, our inspirations, and our dreams today as he spoke to Moses, Aaron, and others in that day. In moments of inspiration we, too, can speak as did our biblical ancestors: "Today God has acted in our lives."

In Friday's text Moses orders Aaron to save a portion of the manna to show to future generations. Though the text speaks of placing the manna in a jar "before the testimony" (the Ark of the Covenant), the writer of Hebrews in the New Testament states that the manna was placed *in* the Ark, along with Aaron's staff and the two tablets of the Law. There is no record of what happened to the Ark of the Covenant after the destruction of the first Temple in 587 B.C., nor to its contents.

The Epistle readings:

1 Peter may have been written by a disciple of Peter, rather than by the apostle himself, since the letter addresses a his-

toric situation of persecution that existed after the apostle's death. A disciple of Peter could have used his teacher's name to add authority to the writing, a common practice of the time. The writing opens in the form of a letter addressed to persecuted Christians living in Asia Minor. Some scholars feel that 1 Peter is actually made up of fragments from an early baptismal liturgy. The writer may have combined the liturgical sections with commentary and admonitions addressed to a church under siege.

1 Peter is an appropriate book to read at this Easter season as we look again at the meaning of our own baptism and concentrate, as a parish family, on the incorporation of the newly baptized into the life of the church. Hear again the admonitions given to the converts of the primitive church. How do they apply to our life situation? Whether or not the words we read are actually sections of an ancient baptismal liturgy, the writing is addressed to the recently baptized who need to be reminded of their baptismal covenant in a time of great trial.

Persecution and struggle are the tests of the Christian. Out of the struggle comes a deeper relationship to Christ who continues to suffer for the redemption of the world through the church.

> In this you rejoice, though now for a little while you may have to suffer various trials, so that the genuineness of your faith, more precious than gold which though perishable is tested by fire, may redound to praise and glory and honor at the revelation of Jesus Christ (1 Pet 1:6-7).

Verses 1-9, read on Monday, may be an early hymn sung at the time of baptism on Easter morning.

One of the accusations made against Jesus as he stood before Caiaphas was that he had been heard to say that he had the power to destroy the Temple and build it up in three days (Matt 26:61). Wednesday's text may reflect those words attributed to Jesus. The new Temple is to be the Christians gathered as the church. The cornerstone of the new Temple will be the risen Christ, a cornerstone that many will trip and fall over because they refuse to believe in the Christ. For those who do believe, however, the cornerstone becomes their way to be part of a royal priesthood, a chosen people.

Psalm 118:22 provided the basis for the writer's thinking, as well as words attributed to Jesus: "The stone which the builders rejected has become the chief cornerstone." The psalmist may have had Israel or one of Israel's kings in mind as he wrote that verse. A nation rejected by other peoples was the nation favored by God and was the chief cornerstone of God's activity in the world. The church quickly applied this metaphor to the risen Lord.

Wednesday's lection also mentions the spiritual sacrifices of the Christian. The eucharistic prayers of The Book of Common Prayer reflect this idea from 1 Peter: "We celebrate the memorial of our redemption, O Father, in this sacrifice of praise and thanksgiving" (p. 363).

Wednesday's reading may have been part of the homily offered to the converts just after their baptism. Slaves and servants must submit to their masters. Everyone must submit to the authority of government. The ill treatment received at the hands of government and master gives the Christian an opportunity to participate in the redeeming suffering of Christ. These postbaptismal admonitions must be read in the light of Christian history, not as commandments for Christians to follow today. The church does not advocate passive acceptance of enslavement and oppression, but the message of 1 Peter is still relevant. Where Christian people suffer for the sake of justice and the gospel, they are participating in the suffering of Christ.

Friday's text contains the one biblical reference to Christ's descent to hell between his death and resurrection. Even those in hell have a chance to repent and turn to the Lord. This concept is expressed in the Apostles' Creed. The only other reference to Christ reaching out to the dead for salvation is found in Acts 2:27, which in turn is a quotation from Psalm 16:10: "For thou dost not give me up to Sheol, or let thy godly one see the Pit." Friday's reading of 1 Peter 3:18—4:6 could be a creedal statement recited by the Christian community at the time of the Easter baptisms.

The Gospel readings:
This week we step into the Gospel of John to look at the words that apply to life in the body of Christ after the Lord's resurrection. Chapters 14-16 are a part of the "farewell discourse" of Jesus, words shared with the disciples at the Last Supper to prepare them for his death and their new life in the Holy Spirit after the resurrection. The choice of this portion of John for the second week of Easter is most appropriate. These words help us to understand our life in the body of Christ today.

Sunday's lection is one of the options suggested for reading at the time of burial. Jesus goes to prepare the way for each one of us. Jesus is the way, the truth, and the life. Anyone who has seen Jesus has seen the Father. The church is to reflect the life of Christ in the coming generations. "Truly, truly, I say to you, he who believes in me will also do the works that I do; and greater works than these will he do, because I go to the Father" (John 14:12). The Holy Spirit was promised by Jesus to the disciples and to the church to empower the church to do the works of the Lord. Moreover, the teaching begun by Jesus will be continued by the Spirit who becomes the new means of revelation to the disciples.

The concern expressed in the epistle readings this week is picked up in the gospel reading assigned for Thursday. As Jesus was persecuted and suffered to proclaim the gospel, so will the church suffer persecution. The world will hate the church, just as the world hated Jesus. Part of the calling of the disciple is to share in that rejection. The Lord's way is not the way of the world, and this leads inevitably to a clash between the church and the world. Popularity and success, as judged by the world's standards, are not the lot of the church, it would seem if we take the words from the Gospel of John seriously.

We conclude our instructions for life in the body of Christ on Saturday. The church is to pray in Jesus' name: "Truly, truly,

I say to you, if you ask anything of the Father, he will give it to you in my name" (John 16:23). This admonition is carried out in every formal prayer offered by the church.

Jesus has spoken in ways that are not always clear, but the time will come when everything will be clear. Paul's familiar words from 1 Corinthians 13:12a—"For now we see in a mirror dimly, but then face to face"—come to mind.

The third week of Easter

The Old Testament readings:

Easter is the season in which the church looks at the meaning of our covenant made with the Lord in baptism. The reading of the Book of Exodus during the Easter season is appropriate for it traces the story of the making of the first convenant with Israel.

Jethro, a priest of Midian and the father-in-law of Moses, had a strong influence on Israel's life in the wilderness. From Sunday's lection we understand that Moses must have left his wife and two children with Jethro during the time of the plagues and Exodus. Jethro reunited the family and offered sacrifices as a priest to the god whom Moses had met at the burning bush. It is interesting to note that a priest of Midian was the first to offer sacrifices to the god of Israel, and it was Jethro who advised Moses on how to expeditiously administer justice for the 12 tribes.

". . .and you shall be to me a kingdom of priests and a holy nation. . ." (Ex 19:6). These are the words that frame our understanding of what it means to be the church of Christ. In calling Israel into covenant, the Lord first rehearsed the mighty acts carried out on Israel's behalf. The covenant was seen as a response to God's action for the nation. Listen to the Prayer of Consecration at the Eucharist and notice the same pattern. First, the mighty acts of God are remembered; then we are called into faithful convenant, expressed in the offering we make and in the sacrament we receive: "We give thanks to you, O God, for the goodness and love which you have made known to us in creation; in the calling of Israel to be your people. . ." (BCP, p. 368).

"On the third day" the Lord "spoke" to Moses, Aaron, and Israel in peals of thunder, flashes of lightning, in a dense cloud, and with the sound of trumpets. This theophany, or appearance of God, is what Israel recreated in the Temple liturgies with the burning of incense, the sounding of the ram's horn, and other ritual acts. Many of our liturgical traditions in the church today grew out of ancient Jewish worship customs practiced in Temple and synagogue. For example, when incense is used in the church it recalls the appearance of God before Israel so that Christians may feel the wonder of that moment happening in their lives. Motifs from Sinai found their way into New Testament writings. Read chapter 2 of Acts; notice how "mighty winds" and "tongues of flame" announce a new covenant as "thunder and lightnings" marked the giving of the first covenant.

The Ten Commandments, or Decalogue, form the heart of the Law outlined in the Torah, or first five books of the Hebrew scriptures. Actually, there are 613 commandments of Torah, but the 10 rehearsed in Exodus 20 provide an outline of the whole fabric of the covenant. Israel is to respond faithfully to God in ritual act, in remembering the mighty acts of God and in responding to God through doing justice to the neighbor and the stranger among them.

Keep the celebration of the Eucharist in mind as you read Friday's text. It is blood poured on the altar and on the people that mark the new covenant. In Exodus 24:9-11 we read that the elders of the tribes ate and drank before the Lord. At the Eucharist we eat and drink before the Lord as a sign that we are part of the convenant people.

The descriptions of seeing and hearing God need not be literalized. Scripture is filled with the language of metaphor and poetry, the only appropriate way to speak of the divine mystery. Israel's identity and covenant was being formed in an encounter on the mountain. The earth may well have shaken from some seismic event, but the people's lives were shaken in this great meeting. That is what is described so powerfully in these chapters.

Israel was to remember the Lord's presence even when they were not standing at the mountain. The making of a portable sanctuary and the Ark of the Covenant were to provide a constant reminder. God would "appear" before Moses and Israel in the Tent of Meeting. God would lead Israel as the Ark was carried in procession before the tribes. The cover, or mercy seat, mentioned in Saturday's reading was seen as the very throne of the Lord. Leviticus 16:1-22 describes how this seat was used as a place where blood offerings were made for the forgiveness of the people's sins. The testimony, or tokens, to be placed in the Ark were the stone tablets. Last week we read that some of the manna was also placed in the Ark as a remembrance of the wilderness wanderings.

The Epistle readings:

Colossians becomes our focus for six days, beginning on Tuesday. Many scholars think that a disciple of Paul actually wrote the letter, using Paul's name as a mark of authority which was an accepted practice of the time. The disciple's work became a commentary on the master's original writings. Paul never visited Colossae. It was Epaphras who converted the citizens. Once the evangelist left the area, however, other teachers introduced contradictory ideas to the converts. We can only catch glimpses of the exact nature of the false teachings since the writer never fully explains them. He assumed his readers were fully aware of the conflict.

Colossians 1:15-20 appears to be a hymn sung by the primitive church. Hymns, liturgical prayers, and even portions of homilies were incorporated into the epistles. The writer appropriated this ancient hymn as a way of reminding readers that Christ is all we need for our salvation. Christ is over and in every aspect of life. We need no other powers to sustain our lives. Apparently the false teaching that was infecting the church of Colossae called for belief in a wide range of angelic beings who mediated between people and God.

Secret religious societies were popular in New Testament times. The fraternity and sorority traditions on college campuses today owe their origins to the ancient mystery religions of biblical times. Salvation meant being initiated into the secrets of a philosophical, religious system. Once the secrets had been divulged, the believer received the benefits of faith. Paul refuted the teaching. The only secret, or mystery, the Christian needs to worry about is "Christ in you, the hope of glory" (Col 1:27).

When Paul used the word, faith, he was speaking of an attitude of total trust in the unseen God who was being revealed in Jesus Christ. "For I am not ashamed of the gospel; it is the power of God for salvation to every one who has faith" (Rom 1:16). Faith, as used by the writer of Colossians, has become a body of knowledge to be accepted or rejected. "As therefore you received Christ Jesus the Lord, so live in him, rooted and built up in him and established in the faith, just as you were taught, abounding in thanksgiving" (Col 2:6-7).

The mystery religions infecting the Colossian church must have emphasized strict ritual practices and extensive codes of self sacrifice and piety. The Christian is not to be bound to such empty practices, the epistle states. We died with Christ as we were "drowned" in the waters of baptism so that we could be raised up with Christ in the resurrection. The empty practices of the religious cults were mere shadows of the true life revealed by Christ.

The Christian must live for the higher order that is being revealed through Christ. The Christian is to "put on" the new garments that are appropriate to wear in the world—compassion, kindness, lowliness, meekness, patience, forebearance, forgiveness, and love (Col 3:12-14). There is a "here, but not yet" quality to this writing. Christians have died to their old nature and put on the new nature of Christ which results in their transformed behavior. But obviously, the Christian still struggles with earthly things, i.e. whatever keeps us from being fully alive in Christ. Christians will be revealed in the fullness of their new nature when Christ is fully revealed in glory. As a priest puts on the vestments for the celebration of the Eucharist, it is symbolic of the putting on of the nature of Christ.

The Gospel readings:

The Easter season is a time of reflecting with joy on the meaning of our baptism. We begin this week with the sequential reading of the Gospel of Matthew. Except for an optional reading of the geneology of Jesus, we move directly to Jesus' baptism, temptations, the calling of the first disciples, and the first mention of his healings.

As you read Matthew this week, recall the Exodus motif from the Old Testament. Just as the first Israel moved through the waters of the Sea of Reeds (or Red Sea) into a time of testing and temptation, so Jesus, the new Israel, moves out of his experience in the waters of his baptism immediately into the wilderness of his trial and temptation. Unlike the first Israel, Jesus does not succumb to the temptations. No golden calf here!

Realize that the picture given of the temptations is poetic imagery and not literal reporting of the event. Jesus is tempted to follow his own will rather than that of the Father, even at the end of his life ("Remove this cup from me . . ." Mark 14:36). Thus we can look at Thursday's reading as a poetic statement of Jesus' struggle to follow perfectly the will of God.

The point of the story is not to be lost on the church, the body of Christ in the world today. Jesus' temptations are ours. The temptations, as Henri Nouwen has said, are to be relevant, spectacular and powerful. (Henri Nouwen, Lectures on Ministry and Spiritual Formation, New Haven, CT.: Paul Vieth Christian Education Service, Yale Divinity, "Temptation," cassette tape #2). That is the seductive siren call that tempts the church time and again. The powers of the present age will acknowledge our relevance and our spectacular power if we who are the church will just give our subservience to them, rather than to the risen Christ.

The Gospel of Matthew was written to provide instruction for a young church beginning to face the reality that the faithful Christian must live for a period of time in the world before the return of Christ at the end of the age. How were they to understand their life in Christ in the present age? Who had authority in the church? How were decisions to be made? How was the covenant revealed through Christ to direct their daily lives? How could they explain their faith in Christ to their friends?

The fourth week of Easter

The Old Testament readings:
Moses' brother, Aaron, was to be the high priest who would stand before the Lord on behalf of the people. His sons would serve as priests under him. The description we read of Aaron's consecration and his elaborate vestments were a source of authority to the high priest who served in later generations. Aaron's sons were seen as prototypes for the other priests of the Temple. The Urim and Thummim mentioned in Sunday's readings were lots cast by the priests on behalf of the people. One of the vestments of Aaron was to be the ephod, a seamless robe that went over the head like a poncho or chasuble. Jews in Jesus' time may have connected his seamless robe worn at the crucifixion, with the high priest's ephod. This was a further symbol of Jesus' role as true high priest acting on behalf of the people.

The familiar story of the golden calf is encountered this week. The punishment for Israel's apostasy was swift. Moses asked for volunteers to punish the people, and the Levites came to his side. They slew 3,000 of the Israelites, the text states, and this act of allegiance to God "consecrated" the Levites before God. In this act of obedience, the authority of the Levitical priests who served in the Temple at Jerusalem was established. The account sounds brutal, but notice that the terrible act of vengeance against the people was inspired by Moses' words, not by words thundered from the heavens. Though Moses undoubtedly felt that he spoke for the Lord, he responded to the situation out of his perception of how God would have him act.

We read in midweek that God's mercy was revealed to Moses in prayer. "Who would guide the apostate Israel through the awesome wilderness?" Moses asked in prayer. The response came clearly. The Lord would lead the nation to the Promised Land. Metaphorical language was used to describe the mystery of Moses' encounter with the Lord in a later scene on the mountain. God would reveal himself to Moses, but that revelation could never be complete. Moses would see only the "backside" of the Lord and not the fullness of the mystery of God.

New commandments were given to Moses in this encounter at Sinai. Read these commandments carefully and compare Exodus 34:14-26 with the commandments found in Exodus 20 that we read two weeks ago. The commandments read this week are a ritual covenant calling for Israel to remain pure and separate from other nations, to keep the three pilgrimage festivals, to dedicate the first-born males to the Lord and to follow other ritual prescriptions.

When Moses brought the tablets of the Law down to the people, his face shone from the close presence of God experienced on the mountain. In Matthew 17:2, we read that Jesus' face shone in his encounter with God on the Mount of Transfiguration.

Our reading of Exodus closes with Moses erecting the Tabernacle in the wilderness. This was a sign before the people that God was personally leading them toward the Promised Land.

The Epistle readings:

The Epistle to the Colossians closes with an admonition to families. Wives were to be subject to their husbands, and husbands were to love their wives. Slaves were to be obedient to their masters as a sign of reverence to God. This listing of family relationships must not be taken as a timeless decree setting forth the structure of families living in today's society. "Husbands and wives be subject to each other" is the understanding of marriage expressed in the Celebration of a Marriage, as set forth in The Book of Common Prayer. Just as we would no longer insist on slaves being subject to a master, we no longer insist on wives being subject to their husbands in the hierarchical fashion of the New Testament times. The writer closes the letter with greetings to the church at Laodicea. In this brief closing statement, we see the way important letters were shared among the churches. An epistle would be read before a congregation, copied and then handed on to other congregations.

Sometimes the copies were not exact, which accounts for variances in the texts that are noted in the margins of some Bibles.

This week, we are exposed to the earliest writing of the New Testament with the reading of Paul's First Letter to the Thessalonians. Acts 17 describes the context of Paul's brief visit in Thessalonika. Paul was on his second missionary journey. He and Silas had just been miraculously saved from imprisonment by an earthquake in Philippi. They then moved on to the city of Thessalonika where they again encountered difficulties with the Jewish authorities. After a short time, Paul was forced to leave the city and wend his way down to Athens and then on to Corinth. Though his visit at Thessalonika was short, Paul stayed long enough to establish a church firmly rooted in the gospel he preached.

While in Corinth (about 50 A.D.), he continued to think about his friends in Thessalonika. He sent Silas and Timothy back to Thessalonika to find out how the young church was doing. They returned to Paul in Corinth with good news—the gospel had indeed taken root, but they also brought back a concern from the people about the "parousia" or return of Christ at the end of the age. "When is the end to come?", the people were asking, "and what happens to those among us who have already died? Will they be taken into the kingdom with Christ, or will they be left behind?" It is this concern for the end of the age that makes the letters to the Thessalonians appropriate for the Easter season.

Read the letter and feel both the hope and the pain that Paul must have felt.

The Gospel readings:

The Sermon on the Mount will be our focus for this week. The writer of the Gospel of Matthew collected many of Jesus' sayings and placed them together in this the first of five great teaching discourses. Here Jesus instructs his disciples on the way to righteousness. Matthew constantly reinforced the theme that Jesus brought the new covenant. Matthew did this in an almost subliminal way by lining up Jesus' actions against the backdrop of the liberation pilgrimage that Moses and the Israelites made from Egyptian slavery to the Promised Land. Just as Moses went up in the mountain to offer the Law, so Jesus goes up on a mountain to instruct his disciples in the new Law. Jesus is a new lawgiver. This is, indeed, the new covenant or the "new testament."

Read Isaiah 61:1-2 for the context out of which Jesus spoke the Beatitudes. The Lord comes to the powerless, to the struggling peoples who know they cannot live by their own power. He comes to those seeking what is right and who are ready actively to oppose what is unjust in society. Those who are now struggling and seeking will be fulfilled in the reign of God. Indeed, they already taste that fulfillment as they sit on the hillside with Jesus.

Matthew 5:17-20 sets the record straight. Jesus did not come to negate the Law and the Prophets. He came to fulfill them. The Torah was felt by the faithful Jew to be the perfect revelation of wisdom to all people. Jesus did not deny the wisdom of the Law. He announced that he had come to deepen the revelation, to move beyond the teaching of Torah. His own life would be a living experience of what the Torah stated in writing. With Jesus, Torah was incarnate, lived out in flesh and blood.

As we read the Sermon on the Mount we discover what Jesus meant about coming to fulfill the Law. The 613 commandments of the Torah set forth for the faithful Jews provided guidelines for every aspect of their lives. The ultimate purpose of life for the Jew was to know and to follow Torah. The commandments were not great burdens to the Jew. They were constant reminders to the faithful of their covenant with God who guided every waking and sleeping moment.

But the commandments of the Law, Jesus would say, were only the top layer of righteousness. One had to go to the heart of the intent of the Torah commandments to truly respond to God's covenant. For example, anger is the root cause for murder. Even to feel anger for another means that one has stepped outside of God's intention for man and woman. Loving one's neighbor, as Torah commands, is only the beginning of what it means to love. We must learn to love our enemy, as well as our neighbor. Jesus' words on the Law speak of a new ethic.

This ethic of the kingdom of heaven makes little sense in terms of the ethic of the present age, but God calls us to live as if the kingdom had already fully come. The church is the forerunner of the kingdom. The church must provide glimpses of what that kingdom will be.

Notice the admonition in Matthew 5:23-24, that we must make peace before going to the altar. We are called in the liturgy of the Holy Eucharist to pass the peace, either at the offertory or right before the administration of the sacrament. The peace is not just a simple greeting between people. It is a vivid reminder of Jesus' words.

The restrictions on divorce that Jesus promulgated need to be read in the light of divorce customs of the time. Under some rabbinic interpretations, a man could divorce his wife with a mere statement of intent. The wife had few protections. Jesus' words gave women some rights. Marriage was not to be taken lightly.

The fifth week of Easter

The Old Testament readings:
This week we move into the third book of the Torah (meaning Law or teaching), the Book of Leviticus, a name taken from the Levitical priests who served at the Temple. If the Lord is to dwell in the midst of the people, how are they to respond to that awesome presence? That is the immediate concern of Leviticus. Though Leviticus may be associated in our minds with an endless listing of ritual prescriptions for the Israelites, it is a significant book for Jew and Christian alike. When we believe that the Lord does indeed dwell in our midst, we must be concerned with our response. Though old Jewish purification laws may not seem relevant to us, the reverence behind those laws is deeply significant to us.

The first seven chapters of Leviticus that are not assigned for our readings, deal with the ritual laws of sacrifice. We begin our reading of Leviticus at the second major division of the book, which deals with the setting apart of "ordained" priests to serve before the Lord at the altar. The high priest, represented by Moses' brother Aaron, is given the most extensive descriptive treatment, but his consecration affected the setting apart of other priests as well. The rituals we read in Leviticus were actually developed over a long period of time. They reflect the practices of the Temple build by Solomon in Jerusalem. The wilderness was seen as the origin of Israel's worship so that all the ritual codes were attributed to that dawning of Israel's consciousness under Moses.

The consecration recounted in Sunday's reading is comparable to the consecration of a bishop or the ordination of a priest in the church today.

The third part of Leviticus deals with the purification of the people, especially after they have sinned. Chapter 16, read on Monday and Tuesday, describes the origins of the Yom Kippur or the Day of Atonement. In the days of the Jerusalem Temple, the high priest would receive two goats. One goat was sacrificed before the Lord, the other goat became the "scapegoat." The sins of the people were symbolically laid on the scapegoat and the animal was led into the wilderness to die. This goat was also known as the goat of the Precipice (New English Bible) or the goat of Azazel, a demon or devil thought to dwell in the wilderness. The high priest then entered within the veil of the Temple and stood before the mercy seat that covered the Ark of the Covenant. He was seen as entering into the very presence of God who "sat" on that mercy seat in the midst of the nation. Burning incense kept the high priest from seeing the mercy seat, since seeing the Lord would have meant instant death for the priest. A bull was sacrificed for the sins of the people and its blood was then sprinkled by the high priest on the mercy seat.

The ritual acts were seen as purifying the people for the sins committed during the year. Read Hebrews 5:1-10 and 7:1—10:18 to see how some Christian writers understood Jesus' mission. Jesus is the perfect high priest whose one sacrifice on the cross cleanses people in all ages. In Christ, there is no more need for continual sacrifice as in the days of the Temple. Christ "cleanses the thoughts of our hearts" even as "all our desires are known and all our secrets are revealed" (BCP, p. 355).

"And the Lord said to Moses, 'Say to all the congregation of the people of Israel, You shall be holy; for I the Lord your God am holy'" (Lev 19:1-2). Israel cannot be a nation like other nations. Israel mlust reflect the utter holiness and righteousness of God. The final section of Leviticus, that we begin on Wednesday, prescribes Israel's holy life before the Lord. Social justice is an immediate concern. These are not just ritual regulations of holiness. If Israel is to be holy, the nation must reflect the justice and compassion of the Lord. The Lord will be seen in the righteous acts of the nation. For example, grain must be left in the field and grapes must be left on the vine for the poor to glean. In summary, ". . .you shall love your neighbor as yourself . . ." (Lev 19:18). Those are the very words that Jesus quoted to remind us that God's holiness is reflected in the lives of faithful people. Jesus incarnated that holiness and justice in his life and in the life he demanded from his followers.

The liturgical calendar of the Jews is set forth in Friday's and Saturday's readings. Reading Leviticus 23 is like reading the calendar of the church year (BCP, pp. 15-18). Listed in order are prescriptions for: Sabbath (23:3); Passover (23:4-14); Pentecost (23:15-22); the Day of Atonement (23:26-32 and Lev 16); and the Feast of Booths or Tabernacles (23:33-44).

The origin of our celebration of Palm Sunday is found in Leviticus 23:40: "And you shall take on the first day the fruit of goodly trees, branches of palm trees, and boughs of leafy trees, and willows of the brook; and you shall rejoice before the Lord your God for seven days." The waving of palms and branches, associated with the feast of Tabernacles, was a reminder that God dwelled with the people in the Temple. When Jesus entered Jerusalem to the waving of palms and went directly to the Temple to cleanse it, he was acting out a statement that led to his crucifixion. "I am God who comes to dwell among you. This is my Temple that I come to cleanse, but I shall raise up a new Temple which will be my church." He was saying this in the way in which he entered Jerusalem.

The Epistle readings:

We conclude the reading of Paul's First Letter to the Thessalonians on Wednesday. Read carefully the description of the day of the Lord. It will come quietly "like a thief in the night" with no signs or warnings.

On Thursday we begin the reading of the Second Letter to the Thessalonians. Many scholars question whether this is a genuine letter of Paul. In Biblical times, it was customary for the disciple of a great teacher to write under his master's name. The language and the imagery of the second letter are certainly different. Notice the strong words of revenge. Those persecuting the church will pay the price in the end. The message about the coming of Christ seems to be a direct contradiction to the first letter. The day won't come as a thief in the night. Rather, the day will be introduced by many dramatic signs.

The Gospel readings:

We continue reading in the sermon on the Mount this week. Monday's admonition on prayer was not meant to denounce all forms of public worship. Humility is the key to prayer. One must avoid acts of officious public piety. The Lord's Prayer is the model prayer for Christians. Note well the petitions that can lose their impact through familiarity. We pray that the kingdom may come "on earth as it is in heaven." It is the ethic of the kingdom, not the ethic of the world that demands our allegiance. We pray for the bread that will sustain us. We have no right for a wealth of bread, only that which we need for the daily life. Then comes the petition of radical forgiveness. To paraphrase: Forgive us to the extent that we are able to forgive others. In Jewish practice one cannot pray for something one is not willing to do.

The temptation or test is the final trial that comes at the end of the age. We pray that we may be spared the anguish of that period of trial and testing. May we be spared from evil, or the evil one, at that moment and at every moment.

The Lord's Prayer is spoken from heaven in the sense that it prays as God would have us pray, rather than as we would conceive of praying. God sees our need in terms of the needs of all humanity. We view prayer from our limited perspective in which we seem to be at the center of the universe. To pray the Lord's Prayer is to see momentarily through the eyes of God.

Familiar words greet us on Thursday: ". . .therefore I tell you, do not be anxious about your life. . ." (6:25). To be a part of the coming kingdom of heaven means a total concentration of responding to God. "Travel light" is the message. The more things we give ourselves to think about, the less we can be a part of the new order. Alcholics Anonymous has a saying that guides the lives of its members: "One day at a time." Take the day, live it fully, and trust that the next day will take care of itself.

The Golden Rule is part of Friday's reading (Matt 7:1-12). A potpourri of Jesus' sayings was collected by the writer of the gospel, sayings about prayer, forgiveness and Christian attitudes in life. "Do not give dogs what is holy" is a saying Matthew inserted into this section. Perhaps Jesus meant "don't burn yourself out on those who do not respond to the gospel."

The sixth week of Easter

The Old Testament readings:
The sabbatical year, familiar from college parlance, owes its origin to Leviticus. Just as every seventh day was to be a day of rest to remember that the Lord rested, so every seventh year was to be a year of rest for the sacred land of Israel. "Volunteer" crops that grew without planting, however, could be eaten as a means of survival.

Moreover, every 50 years (7 years times 7, rounded off to 50) was to be a Jubilee Year (from the Hebrew word meaning the sound of the horn): "And you shall hallow the fiftieth year, and proclaim liberty through the land to all its inhabitants. . ." (Lev 25:10). During this year, any Jew who had become enslaved to another Jew was released, and any Jew who had been forced to sell land could redeem it. This was done so that both land and life would be restored throughout the land. ". . .it shall be a jubilee for you, when each of you shall return to his property and each of you shall return to his family" (Lev 25:10). Though historians seriously question whether the Jubilee Year was ever actually celebrated by Israel, the theological principles that shape the regulations governing the year are still important for every Jew and Christian today.

The Lord brought Israel to her land after rescuing her from enslavement in Egypt. God had shown a compassion that Israel must exercise toward her own people. Justice and care for the poor lay at the heart of Israel's life in covenant with God. Here, aliens were not accorded the compassion, though in other sections of Torah concern for the stranger and sojourner is a principle of justice.

Israel would receive blessings or curses depending on how closely she followed the prescriptions set forth in Torah. The writings many years later of the prophets of Israel and Judah harked back to the demands of the Torah to condemn injustices of the nation that had drifted far from the principles of the covenant.

On Ascension Day, our sequential reading of the Torah is interrupted as we focus instead on readings that deal directly with Christ's eternal reign. (We'll pick up the serial reading of the Torah again in the second week of June with the Book of Numbers.)

The Book of Daniel provides a dramatic scene of God's final triumph over the evil empires of history. This is poetic language and not the literal language of history and prose. The Lord, attended by thousands of thousands, destroys the "beast" (representing the hellenistic kingdom that was such a brutal force in the writer's time). The other three enemy kingdoms are also repressed by God. Then out of the heavens comes "one like a son of man" whom God gives "an everlasting dominion, which shall not pass away, and his kingdom one that shall not be destroyed" (Daniel 7:14). The "saints of the Most High" will "possess the kingdom for ever, for ever and ever" (Daniel 7:18).

This beautiful vision of hope describes the final triumph of the holy ones of God over the evil powers then suppressing Israel. The Lord will finally triumph. God's people will reign in peace and justice forever, and it will be God's power that shall win the victory. The son of man figure was understood in Jesus' time to represent a messianic hope. One man would come, sent by God, to restore God's fallen creation. Christians soon identified this son of man with Jesus. Jesus' own words indicate that he, too, saw this figure as a part of his own identification. In this Old Testament reading, we receive insight into the significance of Jesus' ascension. This feast proclaims that Jesus came into the world to usher in the new age of God, to be culminated in God's final victory over evil, an age when God's people will triumph.

The Song of Hannah (Samuel 2:1-10) is assigned for the day after Ascension Day. This is a triumphant canticle of praise for the God who lifts up the lowly and stands in judgment over all the earth. This is a fitting song of praise for Ascension. The week ends with the description of the giving of the Spirit to the 70 leaders among the 12 tribes of Israel. These men were given a share of God's Spirit bestowed upon Moses, so they could share with him in the guidance of the people. The readings begin to look toward the feast of Pentecost, a week from now.

The Epistle readings:

The epistle readings for Monday, Tuesday and Thursday (Ascension Day) express the theme of Ascension. On Wednesday, Friday and Saturday we begin a sequential reading of the Epistle to the Ephesians.

Monday: We read this selection three weeks ago. Through Christ, we have been "...delivered...from the dominion of darkness and transferred...to the kingdom of his beloved Son" (Col 1:13). In the feast of the Ascension, we recognize that Christ's power extends beyond the domain of this world and this time. Christ represents the kingdom of God that transforms all creation.

Tuesday: "For there is one God, and there is one mediator between God and man, the man Christ Jesus" (Tim 2:5). This text points to another facet of the Ascension. In "ascending" into heaven and "sitting at the right hand of the Father," Jesus becomes our mediator before God.

Wednesday: We begin the sequential reading of the Ephesians. Christ's ascension, celebrated tomorrow, is a reminder that Christ came "...to unite all things in him, things in heaven and things on earth" (Eph 1:10).

Thursday: As we celebrate the feast of the Ascension, it is appropriate to think about the nature of Jesus as both Lord and Savior. Hebrews provides us with a text. The writer of Hebrews is speaking of the fragmentary ways the Lord had spoken to people in earlier times. Angels acted as mediators between human beings and God, but Jesus stands far above angels. With his glorious vision of Jesus in mind, the writer then quotes Psalm 8 to remind the reader that man and woman are "lower than the angels." Despite his place with God, Jesus became fully human and lived a life "lower than the angels." If Jesus is to deliver us from our bondage and lead us to glory, then he must fully identify with our human condition. He must share in our sufferings if he is to redeem them and turn evil to good. The emphasis on suffering was important for a church under persecution.

Friday and Saturday: Ephesians continues from the introduction read on Wednesday. This letter appears to have been written by a disciple of Paul, rather than by the apostle himself. It may have been an introductory statement to the whole body of Paul's letters as they circulated among the churches. Compare Ephesians to Corinthians to see the contrast with a letter known to be written by Paul. In the New Testament times it was common for a disciple to use the name of his mentor. If Ephesians was a cover document for Paul's epistles, it would have been even more natural for a disciple to use Paul's name.

Though the apostle spent considerable time in Ephesus, this epistle lacks a sense of familiarity between the writer and the recipients.

The power of God's free grace revealed in Christ is the theme of Friday's text. We have been created (through our baptism) to carry out the work the Lord has called us to do. We do not act in order to be made righteous before God; our actions for Christ come as a result of the free grace bestowed upon us as disciples.

The generations of enmity and separation between Jew and gentile are ended in Christ. The gentiles who were once far off from God are now brought into union with God through Christ. Jew and gentile are now one. Great words of peace end our week in Ephesians. The follower of Christ becomes a part of the living temple of God.

The Gospel readings:
Monday through Thursday we jump ahead in Matthew's gospel in preparation for Ascension Day. At the ascension, the true nature of Jesus was revealed to the disciples. He was more than a man, more than a healer, more than a teacher. He was God reaching out in a continuing revelation. Monday's and Tuesday's readings are Jesus' parable of the sower and the allergorical explanation of it. The revelation given through the parables helped open the disciples to the revelation of the

ascension. Jesus explained to his disciples that the parables revealed to those who listened, the "secrets" or mystery of the kingdom of God. "To hear the word of and about Jesus, to believe it and act on it, this is the secret of the reign or rule of God in individuals in the Church, and in the world" (*Mark, a Bible Commentary for Teaching and Preaching,* Lamar Williamson, Jr.; John Knox Press, pp. 92-93).

The text for Wednesday may be confusing. Jesus was making subtle use of scripture to make his point. It was thought by many Jews that the Messiah would be a military hero who would reestablish Israel as a major power. The Messiah, moreover, would be a descendant of the great King David. Psalm 110, attributed by the Jews of Jesus' time to King David, reads in verse 1, "The Lord said to my Lord: 'Sit at my right hand, till I make your enemies your footstool.'" "My Lord" was assumed to be the coming Messiah, though that was not the intent of the psalm as originally written. How could King David call his own descendant by the title of Lord? Jesus' point was that the Messiah was to be more than a military hero and more than a descendant of King David. He would indeed be one called Lord, but a Lord who would stand far above kings, prophets, priests or people. "Enlarge your vision of the Messiah," was Jesus' message.

Thursday is Ascension Day and our lection is Jesus' great commission to go forth and baptize in the name of the Trinity. Jesus' life pointed to a reality that exists beyond time, space and temporal creation, and yet a reality that touches every aspect of our lives today. The ascension of Jesus is as much a theological statement as a moment in history. Jesus the man was "lifted up." His ascension raises our life up to a new significance as well. We, too, live in this world, and yet our lives point beyond the present struggle to the realm of God made known to us in Jesus. At Ascension Day our thoughts are directed toward the realm of God, a realm lived out by Jesus and proclaimed as accessible to us.

We read the closing words of the Sermon on the Mount on Friday. *Do* the word is Jesus' final admonition, don't just listen to it. We live for the reign of heaven, not for the reign of the present age. We become radicalized in the sense of being forced to go back and look at the very roots of our response and actions as people. The Christian is to be salt and light in society because the Christian is called to live by a different ethic and value structure. Is it any wonder that we are called to confession and penance as a part of our Christian life?

The seventh week of Easter

The Old Testament readings:
This week, the Old Testament readings are chosen from a variety of books to prepare us for the great Day of Pentecost celebrated next Sunday.

Sunday: Moses is encountered by God at the burning bush. The Lord has identified Moses as one who will work in history and in creation for the liberation and empowerment of Israel.

Monday: That same Lord speaks into the mind of Moses' successor, Joshua. The good news of God's presence with Israel is repeated in the next generation as the people prepare to move, with God's guidance, into the land of Canaan.

Tuesday: The young David is anointed by the prophet Samuel. The pouring of oil on David's head was a sign that God's power and spirit would dwell with him as he became Israel's king. David was to speak and act for the living God of Israel. We are also anointed at our baptism. As the oil is placed on our forehead in the sign of the Cross, the priest says, "you are sealed by the Holy Spirit in Baptism and marked as Christ's own for ever" (BCP, p. 308). Each Christian is called to speak and act for the Lord. We are empowered to do so through the indwelling of the Holy Spirit.

Wednesday: We read words of hope pointing to a time of restoration for the troubled nation of Judah. As a cloud by day and a flame by night guided Israel through the wilderness in the time of Moses, so the Lord's presence will again be seen by the people. They shall know the abiding power in cloud, in flame and in the assurance of shelter and refuge.

Thursday: Zechariah was a prophet who wrote after the people of Judah had returned to their homeland from a generation of exile in Babylonia. From 520 to 515 B.C., the high priest, Joshua, and the high commissioner, Zerubbabel, worked to rebuild the Temple destroyed by the Babylonian armies in 587.

Zechariah wrote in highly symbolic language. The point of today's reading is that it will be God's spirit at work that will accomplish the task of Temple rebuilding. Mountainlike obstacles will be leveled and become like a plain. The Lord, symbolized by the seven lamps, will be ever present in that Temple.

Friday: The Lord will make a new covenant with Israel: "I will put my law within them, and I will write it upon their hearts; and I will be their God, and they shall be my people...they shall all know me, from the least of them to the greatest, says the Lord" (Jer 31:33-34). This new covenant (new testament) was made known at Pentecost (Acts 2:1-13), when the Law of the Lord was indeed written on the hearts of the followers of Jesus, for the Holy Spirit of God entered into those men and women. It is the Holy Spirit who guides and empowers us in the new way of the covenant made through Christ.

Saturday: The theme stated in Jeremiah is continued in the reading from Ezekiel. A new heart and a new spirit will be given to the people. They shall be cleansed by clean water.

Pentecost is one of the five traditional times for baptism in the church today. The clean waters of our baptism prepare us for the power of the indwelling spirit. This reading leads us directly into the experience of the Pentecost celebration. We not only remember the new covenant made with our biblical ancestors, but realize that the covenant is made with us in our own day.

The Epistle readings:

The sequential reading of the Epistle to the Ephesians continues this week. The writer, speaking for Paul, reminds the churches of the great mystery of faith revealed through Christ. All people are to be made one, Jew and gentile alike. In Christ, Jew and gentile are both to have direct access to God. We can know God through Christ.

The practice of offering our prayers "through Jesus Christ, our Lord" comes from the understanding expressed in Ephesians. Tuesday's reading ends with one of the concluding doxologies used in Morning and Evening Prayer: "Glory to God whose power, working in us, can do infinitely more than we can ask or imagine; Glory to him from generation to generation in the Church, and in Christ Jesus for ever and ever. Amen" (BCP , pp. 102 and 126).

The opening versicles for Holy Baptism (BCP, p. 299) are taken directly from Ephesians 4, read on Wednesday: "There is one body and one spirit. . ." This statement echoes the creedal statement of the Jews as they recite the Shema from the Book of Deuteronomy: "Hear, O Israel: The Lord our God is one Lord; and you shall love the Lord your God with all your heart, and with all your soul, and with all your might" (Deut 6:4). The writer of Ephesians proclaims the oneness the Christian can know through Christ.

Wednesday's text quotes from Psalm 68 which the author uses to express the full ministry of Christ: "When he ascended on high he led a host of captives, and he gave gifts to men" (Eph 4:8, paraphrase of Psalm 68:18). Though the psalm speaks of Moses ascending the mountain of Sinai to bring down the gifts of the covenant, the author of Ephesians sees the text as referring to Christ who ascended to the heavens and brought the gifts of the Spirit to the Christians. This imagery from Psalm 68 makes Ephesians an appropriate assignment for the week between Ascension Day and Pentecost.

The gifts of the Holy Spirit enable us to put off the old nature and put on the new. This results in a reorientation of our actions toward Christ. Christians must continue to put on the "complete armor" of the risen Christ if we are to avoid the temptations, the struggles and the entrapments of the present age. As the priest puts on vestments for the liturgy, she or he symbolizes the putting on of the armor of God on behalf of the whole people of God.

The Gospel readings:

To go into the home of a gentile would make a Jew unclean. Can you imagine the shock of the people as they saw Jesus talking to a Roman centurion? Not only was this man a gentile, he was an officer in the army of occupation!

Monday's reading needs to be read in the light of the customs of Jesus' day. Radical things are happening as this Jesus so casually talks to Jew and gentile alike. The miracle is not restricted to the healing of the centurion's servant. The miracle comes partly in an attitude that seems incomprehensible to the established order.

Matthew 8:11-12 refers to the messianic banquet, the metaphor of the reign of God.

There can be no division of commitment, we learn in Tuesday's text. Don't be anxious about the present order, for the kingdom of heaven is breaking into history. Family ties are important, but one cannot wait for a father to die and things to be right at home before going off to follow the path of Jesus. Jesus commands the elements, as well as the attention of men and women. Jesus comes as Savior, one who saves, heals, makes whole again. The prayer of the disciples can be our prayer, too: "Save, Lord, we are perishing" (Matt 8:25).

Wednesday's story tells of Jesus driving demons out of two men (in the Gospel of Mark it is one man), and the demons go into a herd of pigs. We don't use the language of demons to describe mental or physical disorders today, though we have certainly all experienced the sense of being "out of control" at times. Jesus was and is master over that which alienates us from God, from each other, from wholeness. God has the power to heal us. That is the faith we are called to live out as Christians.

The detail about the demons going into the swine would make a good story for a Jewish audience, since swine were anathema to the Jews. The response of the townspeople is one of fear. "This man's power is too frightening for us to handle. Get him out of here," they were saying.

To understand the Pharisee's concern in Thursday's reading, we need to realize that in the Jewish understanding of Jesus' time only God could forgive sins. Temple priests could accept offerings for the forgiveness of sins, but even they could not pronounce the restoration between a person and God. Thus Jesus spoke as God when he stated forgiveness and healing to a paralytic man lowered to him through the roof of a house.

Such a statement would be blasphemy to a Jew. We cannot blame the scribes and Pharisees for their shocked response. Jesus spoke words reserved for God.

Jesus' admonition that new wine cannot be placed in old skins nor new patches be sewn on old clothes concludes our Friday reading. These are words that may slide by our consciousness because of their familiarity. The reign of God, the good news of the gospel, cannot be simply "sewn over" the present system. We cannot adapt ourselves into the old structures where the principalities and powers of the present age hold forth. We must reject the present order and turn to the reign of heaven if we are to know the healing presence of Christ and participate in his reign. The gospel of Jesus Christ is radical; it calls into question all our assumptions about national purpose, economic justice, personal relationships, values and hopes for the future.

The Psalms in the Daily Office

In the Daily Office lectionary we read most of the Book of Psalms in a seven-week cycle if we follow both Morning and Evening Prayer and include the psalms appointed for Sunday. I say most of the psalms, because certain of them are offered as optional readings either because they duplicate canticles found in the rite or because they contain vindictive words calling down God's wrath on the unjust. You will also find that certain verses of some psalms are set off in parentheses with the latter concern in mind. (Lest we condemn the vindictiveness of the Hebrew poets, remember that the desire to crush those whom we consider our enemies is just as strong for us today. It is easy to assume that our enemies are God's enemies, and to pray for a crushing victory over evil.)

As you read the psalms assigned for each day, realize that they are chosen to fit with traditional themes associated with various days of the week and with the time of day. Morning psalms sometimes reflect the feelings associated with awakening to a new day, while evening psalms prepare the reader for a peaceful night of sleep under God's protection.

Psalm 119, the longest of the psalms, is read either in the morning or evening each Wednesday. It is a psalm that praises God for the commandments of the Torah.

Friday's psalms reflect the penitential mood long associated with that day, while Sunday's psalms are apt to be joyful psalms of praise and thanksgiving reflecting the weekly remembrance of the resurrection. (The church since earliest times has taken the Hebrew psalms and adapted them to the Christian calendar.)

Psalms appointed for Saturday evening, on the other hand, tend to deal with themes of creation or deliverance, since Saturday in both Jewish and Christian calendars is the day that God is remembered as having rested upon the completion of creation (Gen 2:1-2). Thus tradition plays an important role in psalm selection. These ancient metaphors and feelings associated with the various days of the week are also carried out in the canticles and collects assigned for the days of the week.

With these thoughts in mind, the following chart is offered so that you can more easily follow the seven week cycle of psalm reading. The initials by each psalm number indicate the type of psalm appointed for each day:

pl—personal lament

cl—lament offered by the psalmist on behalf of the entire community

pr—hymn of praise, probably offered within the context of liturgical worship in the way that we sing hymns as a part of our worship today

prz—hymns of praise for God's city of Jerusalem

pra—hymns of praise that celebrate God's reign over Israel

tr—psalms of trust in God

th—psalms of thanksgiving

ro—royal psalms expressing the feelings and concerns of Israel's kings

w—wisdom psalms that express what it means to be wise in the eyes of God

lit—psalms specifically used as a part of the Temple liturgy; for example, Psalm 24 was used as an entrance ritual at the gates of the Temple

h—psalms that recall Israel's history

to—psalms that express love for the Torah, or Law of God, as written in the first five books of the Old Testament

j—psalm of judgment

As you begin your reading of the Daily Office each week, match up the psalms appointed for Monday with the psalm chart to see which week in the psalm cycle you are in. Glance at the psalms appointed for each day to get an idea of the type of psalm you will be reading. Let your imagination take you back to the original setting of the psalm. If it's a personal lament, see if you can identify with the psalmist's plight. You don't need to know all the details. Just let the words enter your consciousness and identify with the feelings expressed in the psalm. If the psalm expresses thanksgiving, picture the faithful assembled in the Temple giving praise to God, and let that thanksgiving express your feelings of joy in God's presence.

The seven-week cycle is interrupted from the fourth week of Advent through the feast of the Epiphany, around Ash Wednesday, and during Holy Week and Easter Week. Psalms that reflect the mood of those significant days are read instead.

All of the psalms express a common theme: We are utterly dependent on God who is known both as creator and savior/liberator of the people. The collect for the third Sunday in Lent expresses the psalmist's feelings well: "Almighty God, you know that we have no power in ourselves to help ourselves; Keep us both outwardly in our bodies and inwardly in our souls, that we may be defended from all adversities which may happen to the body, and from all evil thoughts which may assault and hurt the soul..." (BCP, p. 218).

The following chart is based on the treatment of the psalms given in *The Jerome Biblical Commentary* (Prentice Hall, Inc. Englewood Cliffs, N.J., ed. by Raymond E. Brown, Joseph A. Tizmeyer and Roland E. Murphy, 1968) pp. 569-602.

Psalms in Daily Worship

	WEEK I	WEEK II	WEEK III	WEEK IV	WEEK V	WEEK VI	WEEK VII
MONDAY							
Morn Prayer	1w, 2ro, 3 pl	25 pl	41th, 52 pl	56pl, 57 pl	80 ol	89:1-18 ol	106:1-18 ol
Eve Prayer	4 pl, 7 pl	9th, 15 lit	44 ol	64pl, 65 pra	77 pl	89:19-52ol	106:19-48 ol
TUESDAY							
Morn Prayer	5 pl, 6 pl	26 pl, 28 pl	45 ro	61 pl, 62 t	78:1-39 h	97 pra, 99 pra	121 tr, 122 pra; 123 ol
Eve Prayer	10 pl, 11 tr	36 pl, 39 pl	47 pra, 48 pra	68 pra	78:40-72 h	94 ol	124 th, 125 tr; 126 ol
WEDNESDAY							
Morn Prayer	119:1-24 to	38 pl	119:49-72 to	72 ro	119:97-120 to	101 ro, 109 pl	119:145-176 to
Eve Prayer	12 lit, 13 pl; 14 pl	119:25-48 to	49 w	119:73-96 to	81 lit, 82 j	119:121-144 to	128 w, 129 ol; 130 pl
THURSDAY							
Morn Prayer	18:1-20 ro	37:1-18 w	50 lit	71 pl	34 w	105:1-22 h	131 tr, 132 ro
Eve Prayer	18:21-50 ro	37:19-44 w	8 pra, 84 pra	74 ol	85 ol, 86 pl	105:23-45 h	134 pra, 135 pra
FRIDAY							
Morn Prayer	16 tr, 17 pd	31 th	40 th, 54 pl	69 pl	88 pl	102 pl	140 pl, 142 pl
Eve Prayer	22 pl	35 pl	51 pl	73 th	91 tr, 92 th	107:1-32 th	141 pl, 143 pl
SATURDAY							
Morn Prayer	20 ro, 21 ro	30 th, 32 w	55 pl	75 lit, 76 pra	87 pra, 90 ol	107:33-43 th	137 ol, 144 ro
Eve Prayer	110 ro, 116 th; 117 pra	42 & 43 pl	138 th, 139 pra	23 tr, 27 pl	136 pra	108 th	104 pra